THE
PENNSYLVANIA
RAILROAD

1940s–1950s

THE PENNSYLVANIA RAILROAD

1940s – 1950s

DON BALL, JR.

Printed in Japan at
Dai Nippon.

Published by Elm Tree
Books, Inc., P.O. Box 396,
Chester, Vermont 05143

Distributed to the general
trade by

W. W. Norton &
Company, Inc.
500 Fifth Avenue
New York, New York 10110

First Edition

ISBN 0-393-02357-5

**A Note on the
Photographs**

All photo credits in this
book correspond to the photographs in the following
sequence: left-hand page,
top to bottom; right-hand
page, top to bottom. Where
all photographs on a page
are taken by the same photographer, only one name
appears in the credits.

To the men and women of the Pennsylvania Railroad Company, and the great nation they have served.

Acknowledgments

Although this book is primarily a trackside look at the locomotives and trains of the Pennsylvania Railroad, I have tried to portray the "flavor of the Railroad" through historic facts, anecdotes, personal recollections, and interviews with PRR employees. At all times, I have tried to use official Company designations, spelling names, classifications, etc., the way the PRR did. Many people have helped me with this endeavor. In all cases, everyone I have called upon has been gracious and I am deeply indebted to them.

I honestly believe that without the strong support and help from Tom Harley, Frank Tatnall, and Dave Sweetland this book may not have materialized. I have known Tom since 1960 when we were in the Pennsylvania Railroad's 717th Railway Operating Battalion and the friendship has grown stronger over the years. Tom's wonderful photographic documentation of the war years, alone, was of tremendous importance, as was his thorough knowledge of mechanical details.

Frank Tatnall was the recipient of more calls from me for help than anyone, and I appreciate his patience, and likewise, his friendship. Frank may also have more pictures in this book than anyone (I have not bothered to count) and if so, for good reason. The photography speaks for itself.

Dave Sweetland, another good friend from the 717th, kept me straight on the diesels (I tend to ignore diesel data, even after all of these years), supplying great photos.

Finally, no part of the vast PRR system and operations confused me more than those within New Jersey. I am convinced Frank Kozempel knows every spike and tie plate in the Garden State and I am grateful to him for sharing his knowledge.

I am indebted to all of the photographers, and I'm forever thankful for those who not only stand at trackside to document the railroads, but who are willing to share their talents for posterity. The following photographers have my thanks: Frank Tatnall, Tom Harley, Dave Sweetland, Dave Cope, Frank Kozempel, Marv Cohen, John Prophet, Jim EuDaly, Charlie Kring, Dick Baldwin, Gordon Lloyd, Jack Raymus, Al DiCenso, Louis Marre, Joe Thompson, Walt Grosselfinger, Al Holtz, Jerry Landau, Eugene Van Dusen, Charles Mahan, Earl Brown, Alvin Schultz and Tom Scholey. I am also grateful to Skip Clark, Don Pope, Frank Zahn, Emery Gulash, and Jim Caldwell. And I certainly want to thank Dave Oroszi for the use of some fine color slides from his collection.

Many other people were of instrumental assistance to me, helping with a wide range of requests and problems. I want specifically to head off this list with Don Hess and Walt Keely of the Pennsylvania Railroad Technical & Historical Society. My search for a color shot of a Q2 in action began with the blase attitude that certainly many early color photographers must have shot some of the twenty-five Q2s out in Ohio and Indiana. Several letters and phone calls led to a more urgent search—and finally an almost frantic trip from Crestline to Fort Wayne, following leads, all to no avail. Walt Keely unexpectedly stumbled across a Q2 picture that led me to Joe Thompson in Texas. And, I might add, after I had hand-colored some Q2 shots out of pure desperation that were printed from negatives shot by Allen Bowers. Walt Keely also came up with some of the dynamometer information I was searching for, on tests of PRR locomotives on the N&W. Many thanks go to Tom Dixon for

6

similar dynamometer test results of the PRR T1s on the C&O. It is my hope someone will do a whole book someday on one railroad's locomotives that were operated and tested on other railroads.

Appreciation goes to my good friend Dick Carpenter, who shares my love of interlocking towers and plants. Whenever I needed information on towers, or simply confirmation of my own records, Dick was there with the information. And in a similar vein, if a question came up concerning signalling, Nelson Bowers was the one with the answers.

Deserving special mention are many more people who answered specific questions, introduced me to others whom I called or visited, or who just offered to help. Hoping I am not leaving anyone out, I want to thank Jay Williams (ayah!), Doug Taylor, Fred Shaeffer, Ray Goodman, Dick Heiler, Al Holtsinger (Altoona Mirror), Ted Mair (Altoona Chamber of Commerce), Skip Sassmannshausen, Allen Bowers, Dick Adams, Roger Keyser, Tom Marsh, Harry Bailey, Bob Schmidt, Clarence Weaver, Elmer Steuernagel, Charlie Feather, Bob Mehlenbeck, Terry Cassidy, Fred Schnieder, and Karl Lich.

Undoubtedly the biggest joy in the course of this project (and one of the most expensive, phone bill-wise) was the countless hours I spent listening to retired railroaders' memories. What riches they hold. I wish I had more pages to preserve everything they said. Again, with great trepidation that I not leave anyone out, my heartfelt thanks go to Eddie Wertz, Paul Mumaugh, Bob Fredericks, Bob Stettler, Lloyd Morris, Jack Moody, Ken Reed, Homer Spires, and Arthur Bixby. Why, just listening to Paul Mumaugh recalling the four-car test train with an E6 taking Warsaw, Ind. at 106—and meeting the Milwaukee *Hiawatha* on a test run no less—is worthy of an entire book!

Finally I get down to a "team" of very special people who have beared with me, and have made this effort possible. First, and foremost, my wife, Linda, who did most of the typing and listened to my "tuscan tongue" for months on end. Likewise, my daughter Whitney (who is the other railfan in the family) and my son, Fenner. I am greatly appreciative for Jeremy Townsend's editing and her understanding that the CT-1000 is a Bible, and that diesels get the hyphens, and not the steam or electrics, etc. Many thanks to Mark La Riviere and Katy Homans for their work on the book, and, for their patient understanding of my fetish for keeping trains in scale with each other, and in size/relation with the distance from the viewer, etc., etc.

I will end this with special thanks to my mom for her lifelong support and understanding of my love for trains. To Jim Boyd, editor of *Railfan & Railroad* for his pointers and help, and likewise to John Earley of Carstens. And to Jim Mairs of W. W. Norton & Company, the distributors of this book to the general trade, my special thanks and gratitude.

D.B.

Introduction

It has been said that in the years preceding the Great Depression, if someone in the Philadelphia business community were to speak of the "President," it had to be made clear whether he meant the current resident of the White House or the chief executive of the "Standard Railroad of the World." While the Pennsylvania constituted only four percent of the U.S. route mileage, its multi-tracked main lines and branches carried over ten percent of U.S. railroad business and its influence in railroad circles was even greater.

When it came to the vision plus the financial and engineering strength to carry out $100 million projects, such as the New York tunnels and terminals (and supporting facilities) and the intercity electrification projects of 1928–38, no railroad was its equal. The immensity of a $100 million project such as the New York improvements in the dollars of 1900–1910 placed it second only to the Panama Canal Project. In terms of today's dollars with inflation plus costly regulatory requirements, it would be a project far larger than any attempted by a railroad in recent years – no doubt billions of dollars.

The electrification project, done in part with federal RFC money promptly repaid, enabled the Pennsylvania to weather the traffic surge of World War II, as it had been unable to do in World War I. Thus a second nationalization was not necessary. It is not difficult to contemplate what permanent damage might have been done to the entire U.S. railroad industry, if it had had to endure a second nationalization in a span of little more than twenty years.

While most of the operating benefits of these two projects now fall to Amtrak and the commuter authorities, the benefits to the public are immense and are no doubt irreplaceable in today's business and political climate.

On the technical development side of the railroad business the Pennsylvania was preeminent in such diverse areas as air brakes, automatic couplers, friction draft gears, modern signalling and the use of steel for rail, wheels and freight and passenger car construction. All of these items are taken for granted today but each represented a significant investment when it was made. The Pennsylvania also pioneered in such diverse business areas as air transport, motor trucking, bus operation and freight containerization. Some of these developments were ahead of their time and some met with regulatory barriers that have only recently been lowered.

The Pennsylvania's leadership in the formation of the Trailer Train Company in 1955 ensured that intermodal rail transportation would flourish. This area is now the most rapidly expanding sector of the railroad business, long after the Pennsylvania has ceased to exist.

Yet despite all that the Pennsylvania accomplished, the railroad got off to a late start when compared to the B&O and other early railroads. The problem was that the State of Pennsylvania had bet its money on the wrong project: its System of Public Works consisting of canals, inclined planes and antique railroads. Passage over this system required five days and a good deal of luck to travel between Philadelphia and Pittsburgh. The chief problems included numerous transfers, passage through hundreds of locks, frozen waterways in the winter, flooded waterways in the spring and all sorts of technical problems involving the operation of ten inclined planes over the Allegheny Ridge at Blair Gap. While other canal systems had been quite successful, witness the Erie Canal which was pushed by New York. The Erie Canal utilized the flat Mohawk Valley and did not have to cross a 2,300 foot mountain ridge.

Pennsylvania's (and Philadelphia's) problem was that it would surely have been beaten out in trade to the West by New York and by Baltimore with its B&O Railroad. The B&O was already eyeing access to Pittsburgh via Cumberland, Maryland, so Pennsylvania had no choice but to charter the Pennsylvania Railroad and seal the doom of its $40 million boondoggle.

The new railroad had the wisdom to hire as its first chief engineer (later president) John Edgar Thomson, the greatest name in the 122-year history of the railroad. Thomson made

the final location, supervised its construction and later developed it into a system that by his retirement in 1874 had reached the general limits of its territory. When you consider that in 1840 Chicago had a population of 4,470 while cities that were heavily involved with water transportation, such as Cincinnati, had a population ten times greater, the major impact the construction of railroads had on shaping the United States of today is evident.

The final irony of the Pennsylvania System of Public Works was that the failure of one of its dams on South Fork Creek many years after the system was abandoned was the primary cause of 2,000 deaths in the Johnstown Flood of 1889.

Over the years the Pennsylvania has been criticized for not designing a successful steam locomotive after the M1a of 1930. The truth is that the intercity electrification and the Great Depression obviated the need for more steam locomotives until World War II, at which time the railroad was required to build proven designs. They made an excellent choice, the C&O 2-10-4, which became 125 class J1 and J1a locomotives built at Altoona between 1942 and 1944. The later construction in 1945 and 1946 of production quantities of duplex locomotives (50 T1 and 25 Q2), while hardly a success story, was of little importance in the overall motive power requirements of a railroad that had over 4,500 steam locomotives.

Another criticism concerns the reluctance of the Pennsylvania to utilize Traffic Control Signalling (TCS), even though a pioneering installation of Centralized Traffic Control existed at Limedale, Indiana in 1930. Evidence of this is shown by the fact that as late as the 1950s, 113 towers stood between Penn Station, New York and Union Station, Chicago.

It can only be said that other financial needs took priority. Some of them, such as the Pittsburgh Passenger Station improvements, not too wisely in an era when cash flow from operations was inadequate to fund needed road capital improvements and external financing for such projects was difficult to obtain. This priority for roadway improvements has been met only in more recent times by Conrail – as ultimate successor to the Pennsylvania and other bankrupt eastern railroads – initially with the assistance of government funding under the 3R and 4R acts of 1973 and 1976, respectively, and NERSA (The Northeast Rail Service Act).

Organizationally the Pennsylvania had a consistency matched by few companies of any type. It was generally headed by a team with strong engineering orientation. The best engineering talent in the country gravitated toward the railroad in the nineteenth century because it was the premier industry. When the U.S. Government was looking for someone to head up the Panama Canal Project at the turn of the century, they chose a railroader, John Stevens, with a background similar to J. Edgar Thomson's – that of locating engineer. When General Pershing, in 1918, asked for the ablest man in the country to reconstruct key parts of the French railroads, the Pennsylvania's W. W. Atterbury (later president) was the choice.

The Pennsylvania paid a continuing dividend to the last, even during the Great Depression. In some years the dividend was not self-generated. (I can recall one year when the dividend was $19 million, although little or no money was generated from operations. Instead, the money came from N&W stock, held by the Pennsylvania Railroad, which paid a dividend of $19 million that year.)

The Pennsylvania Railroad never suffered a bankruptcy and generally avoided the shenanigans such as stock manipulations associated with the robber barons of the railroad industry. It could and did act high-handedly as demonstrated by President A. J. Cassatt's eviction of Western Union by cutting down all of its telegraph poles the night of May 21, 1903. In another story Cassatt is alleged to have responded to an irate passenger on the Main Line whose party was passed up by a commuter train late one night, "That will never happen again, sir." It never did; Cassatt had the station demolished.

Cassatt, however, was also responsible for accelerating the growth of the railroad into a super railroad with multiple tracks and routes, and – something rare in American railroading – multi-level interlockings, such as *Zoo* Tower in Philadelphia, enabling trains to make movements over a number of routes without delaying other trains. The New York improvements were Cassatt's legacy, although he didn't live to see them completed. Samuel Rea, a chief engineer (and later president) handled the New York project. Both Cassatt and Rea were honored by statues erected in Penn Station after their deaths.

I had the honor of serving the Pennsylvania from 1949 until the merger in 1968 and with its successor railroads until 1979. While serving as the Pennsylvania's last assistant chief mechanical officer-locomotives, it was my duty to replace much of the motive power that had been acquired in the first wave of dieselization. The biggest problem locomotives, such as the Baldwin Centipedes and the FM Erie Builts, were already gone, so it became my task to replace Baldwin Sharks, FM C-Liners and Train Masters, Alco PA and RS locomotives and later even EMD E and F units, along with myriad yard switchers of all types. The name of the game was to run the life out of this power and get rid of it just as it breathed its last.

On the electric locomotive side, the P5s had already been replaced by the E44s, so the GG1s had to be placed in a long cannibalization cycle, where the death of a single GG1 produced all sorts of useable components for the remaining fleet. After all, parts for a GG1 were not available in cardboard boxes as were those for the diesels.

I also witnessed some of the less publicized events of the era such as the night in the early 1960s when we took a coal train through the New York tunnels with three E44s on the point. While we showed that it could be done, the slack action was violent due to the extreme vertical curvature of the tunnels and station. When the New Haven attached four Alcos at *Harold* and started over Hell Gate Bridge, a coupler pulled out, undoubtedly due to the shaking we had given the train.

On another occasion we operated what was at the time the world's largest train from Whiskey Island (Cleveland) to Mingo Junction, Ohio (341 cars; 35,805 tons) on September 21, 1967. While we again showed that it could be done, the slack action cost us thirteen knuckles on the rolling terrain.

I assisted on the Metroliner Project, finding out early in my career that political timetables and technical progress are not necessarily compatible. The Metroliner Project was eventually successful, but at a painful cost involving extensive retrofit, starting delays and the necessity of placing technicians on board to ensure that problems could be handled expeditiously. The chief culprits were a development timetable built around President Johnson's reelection (which never occurred due to the Vietnam turmoil) and unrealistic specifications from the Office of High Speed Ground Transportation in Washington.

We used to have annual events that we accomplished with much success such as the well-publicized annual Army–Navy game which involved a spectacular train movement and a less publicized car movement involving the handling, storing and servicing of approximately 65 private passenger cars for the Kentucky Derby. This project required weeks of preparation so that the VIPs attending the event were well "cooled," well "lit" and well "oiled." Any mistake could be detrimental to one's career when handling this group. A list of their names read like the "Who's Who" in U.S. business.

While my duties involved primarily equipment, I could not help but observe the physical plant that had been built by my predecessors. Such places included the multi-track main line over the Allegheny ridge at Gallitzin where the drone of diesels rarely ceased. The main line 11 KV single-phase 25 cycle electrification was "one of a kind" with its tremendous redundancy fed by multiple sources and tied together with 132 KV transmission lines. It has stood the test of time without major interruption for fifty years, enduring hurricanes, floods and even the cessation of supply by a major utility source. The magnificent stone arch bridges, like the world's longest at Rockville, Pennsylvania, which has carried the traffic for eighty years and has withstood the awesome floods and ice jams of the Susquehanna, continue to be one of the many irreplaceable assets of the property.

On the negative side the experiences of train wrecks (some of which made national headlines), fires, storms, floods, the deaths of colleagues in accidents are among the things that railroad operating people face. Few, however, would trade careers. Even the trauma of the Penn Central bankruptcy was met as a challenge to be faced and finally overcome.

It is this feeling of railroading that Don Ball, whom I have known for over twenty-five years, brings to life in his books, including this volume honoring that which was once known as "The Standard Railroad of the World."

—E.T. Harley

History and Recollections

The cabbie seemed to have the knack of it, just making the yellow lights, dodging the slower trucks, buses, and out-of-town drivers as we head (bolt, rather) down 7th Avenue. This is the beginning of the afternoon frenzy as over 3,000,000 human beings start their trek out of Manhattan, running, criss-crossing, cutting in and out to get to their busses, subways, and trains and whatever else it takes to get out of the city. Next to us are other cabs racing along, doing what we are doing, and *somehow* not colliding. People are dashing across in front of us, ignoring crosswalks and lights. Delivery bikes mingle with vehicles as do the guys pushing garment racks. As we near Penn Station, I feel secure that we are going to make it after all, without hitting anyone or anything. I relax my grip on the door handle and the camera bag. In all directions, there are old nondescript buildings laced with fire escapes and topped with funny, squat wooden water tanks. Pizza parlors seem to be everywhere, and a Greek luncheonette is always within sight. There are discount photo supply stores up every cross street along with countless bars, garment places and delicatessens. In the next block, and set back from the street, is the massive Pennsylvania Station with its endless line of Doric columns and stately iron lamp posts. Huge sandstone eagles peer down upon the city. "Seventh Avenue in front will be fine," I say, gaping at the big, bold, austere architectural masterpiece. How so many people can maneuver so quickly in and out of that one station door never ceases to amaze me. But that's Manhattan.

"That will be a dollar five," the cabbie says. A heck of a lot of money just to come over from Grand Central, but I didn't have time to do the Times Square shuttle, change to the 7th Avenue local routine, and then fight the crowds in the small subterranean, shop-filled corridors that lead to the downstairs of Penn Station.

The big entrance clock indicates 4:10 PM—at least twenty minutes later than I was planning. It's me against the world, as I immerse myself into the crowd, almost walking into a big, red-faced cop on the beat around the station. Somehow, the ever-present pigeons stay out from underfoot, finding popcorn in the process. I rush past the fast-moving yet orderly lines of commuters clutching brief cases, buying newspapers on the run, and slapping the folded papers up under their arms. I by-pass the lines and head into the station.

Through the long Italianate vaulted arcade and down the stairs that are faster than the parallel escalators I go until I come to one of the ticket windows "for coach passengers," that seems almost out of place in the great 150-foot high waiting room patterned after the Roman Baths of Caracalla. I purchase a *return* ticket from Philadelphia and do not take time to explain why I do not need a ticket *to* Philadelphia. In my coat pocket is the release and letter good for the one-way passage in the cab, from Ralph C. Champlin, vice president in charge of public relations for the Pennsylvania Railroad.

There is magic in the huge train concourse of Penn Station! Inspired by the great buildings of ancient Rome, particularly the Basilica of Constantine, the enormous area is a constant hubbub of people. Great steel columns soar to a vaulted roof of iron and glass, and there is a wondrous thunder of trains arriving and departing, accompanied by their ringing bells. People are coming and going in all directions, and in the background the constant authoritative voice continues with the announcements of trains. "Local train to Trenton west gate Track 16." In seconds, the rumble of a train coming in from the east fills the room, punctuated by the melodic brass bell of a GG1. "Southbound Congressional to Washington departing at 4:30 West Gate track 12. Passengers to Philadelphia, Wilmington, Baltimore, and Washington, West Gate track 12. This train has coaches, dining car and parlor cars to Washington locations 1731, 1732, 1733, 1734. West Gate track 12."

Unlike the vast openness of the station above track level, down on the platforms it is dark and confining. At once you are part of the working railroad. I hold up a line of pin-striped businessmen as I explain to a couple of trainmen that I am to ride the head end. I walk beside the gleaming train towards the head and locate the conductor. Under a flashlight, he reads the letter, glances at the accompanying release signed by J. W. Leonard, superintendent of passenger transportation, Eastern Region. He looks me in the eye and tells me I'd be a lot more comfortable back in the train. I am quickly introduced to the engineer, Ray Clayton, and fireman, brother Russ Clayton, *and* to GG1 #4909, clean tuscan, and gold. Both Claytons make me feel that I belong. The great GG1 motor is inanimate; the humming auxiliary motors are the only hint of her being energized. Up ahead, the sun glares down on the opening between the post office and station, reflecting off the silver rails and traceries of overhead wires back into the darkness. Ray Clayton tells me to get on if I want to go with them. The conductor walks back towards the bottom of the stairs and waits for the attendant to "give them the gate" at 4:30. The last passengers hurry down the stairs and into the nearest cars. A tower is notified that No. 153 is ready. Within a matter of seconds, two whistles from the communication line pierce through the cab. The nearby pot signal goes to a *slow-clear.*

At precisely 4:31 PM, we start to ease the 18-car train out of Penn Station "as smooth as velvet." Ray advances the 22-notch controller one notch at a time accompanied by the loud, disconcerting BOP! BOP! of the transformer tap switches. We nose out into the sunshine and are treated to the magnificent sound of our twenty wheels clacking over the cross-overs and through a double-slip switch. Twelve pinions running against six gears driving six double-ended quills and twelve drivers move this great machine. Since the twelve motors are bolted to the frame, we can literally feel their every vibration. The steel-on-steel parade is simply magnificent! Engineer Clayton eases the controller open another notch, accompanied by the loud pop of the tap switches. He's sensitive at every moment to the G, the train and the intricate track work. As quickly as we got out of the dark of Penn Station, we enter darkness somewhere under 10th Avenue, lined onto No. 2 track leading to the tunnel. The cab signals blink on *clear* as we enter cab signal territory.

In the tunnel, everything is much louder—the hum of traction motors, clack of the wheels and snap of the tap switches amplify the fact that this graceful machine really has power. The speed quickly increases as we head down under the Hudson River. Now, the wind starts to rush through the cab. Whatever else people say about the GG1, the cab was not designed to accommodate extra riders. Talking in the tunnel is absolutely impossible, and the closeness of the tunnel and bench walls makes the confinement in the cab, which is built within the bridge-truss framework of the car body, seem even tighter. The powerful G is pushing a bow wave of air ahead of us now; the rush of the vacuum pops my ears from the loss of air pressure. The rear pan is now riding only a couple of inches above its latch-down position—no room to spare. We are at the bottom of the vertical curve deep under the river and the GG1 really starts to show its stuff. There is a hint of train resistance as we begin the uphill climb. Ray Clayton watches his three overloads, set to trip at 2700 amps per circuit and reaches for another notch every time the current decays. This incredible machine has an overload output in excess of 8000 horsepower, but with today's train *that much power* is not needed. In a matter of seconds, Ray leans on the whistle cord to the deep resonant horn to warn that we're going to exit the tunnel at speed. There's a *whomph!* And we are out in sunlight. Ray starts to notch out, answered by the popping tap switches. There is an impatient look in his eyes, as we head out of the curve and into the tangent. I glance back at our beautiful stainless steel train following us around the curve like a trailing ribbon. In front of the observation three heavyweight parlor cars interrupt the sweep of our silver train. Beyond the gray, brown, and dingy green of Bergen Hill is the New York skyline. "Clear!" calls the fireman, Russ. "Clear!" Ray answers.

Number 1 pantograph stretches up to the web-like wires overhead as it silently tears at the 11,000 volt trolley. The great G cruises on the tangent (what other locomotive cruises?), the trailing cars seemingly an afterthought as we glide down the rails, like a child's wagon hooked to a car's bumper. We roar over steel deck bridges over road after road, and over other railroads, on twin rails boxed in by catenary poles, transmission wires and overhead contact wires. The geometric patterns of the wires and supports rushing by are hypnotic. Headlights appear and we close in on each one in a *whoosh*! Every twenty-four hours 475 passenger trains and 120 freight trains roll over the New York-Washington tracks. We are certainly riding over what is probably the most phenomenal piece of railroad in the world! "Clear." Russ yells. To my immediate left, and next to Russ are the position light cab signals that display and duplicate the wayside signals governing our track. They can display *clear, approach-medium, approach,* and *restricting speed* aspects. Our lights are lit straight up and down as we roar down the track.

At Philadelphia, I have one hour to kill and Liggetts Drug Store's soda fountain in 30th Street Station hits the spot. One hamburger and a chocolate shake are followed by another burger and another chocolate shake. (I quickly add this counter to my location list for "all time best chocolate shakes.")

On the 7:00 *Clocker* to New York, I grab a window seat on the "railroad side" of the car. I had been treated to my first real taste of PRR "standard railroading" and I loved every bit of it! As we head back toward New York, I ponder the Pennsylvania Railroad, what I love about it, and what I loathe about it. I realize that the PRR is one of the few major railroads of which I have had very little first-hand knowledge or hands-on experience. One thing is crystal clear: the Pennsylvania is an entity to itself, and it is *different*. It is a railroad that many people love, and perhaps, an equal number of people love to hate. Perhaps this comes with the size. The P-70 I was in was basic in all respects, built in the Altoona Shops as the standard Company design for passenger cars. Over a period of thirty-one years, more than 1,460 of them were built before the first lightweight P-82 coach in 1938. The semi-rounded bulkhead door, finished off with a typically Pennsy curve, has always bothered me from the standpoint of aesthetics. The slightly garish no smoking sign that was stuck in the metal doorway molding didn't smooth the rough edges. But we were moving! Traveling at incredible speeds, and isn't that what a railroad that happens to be in the most densely populated part of the country should be doing?

I turn back to the great electric boulevard of steel out my window and fix my eyes on the lovely pink towering cumulous clouds over the Jersey Meadows. The web of catenary and transmission lines zing past, punctuated by train after train. The roadbed is beautiful and the hard-riding, not-so-quiet P-70 coach rolls solidly along behind our GG1. And what a tribute the GG1 is to the genius of Pennsy! To have selected and operated one class of engine to handle the trains along the busy corridor for so many years, with no need for replacement. The GG1's very lines suggest sturdiness, stamina, and speed. I think about the great cab ride I took earlier today, and I wonder where Ray and Russ are at this moment. It's wonderful that the Clayton family men are all working for the Railroad, enjoying their work, and each other. I wonder why it is that railroaders in engine service seem to be so forthright and good-natured. I turn my head back towards the window, watch the rails, catenary, passing trains, and doze off.

During the 1850s and the ensuing decades there was much talk of getting a railroad bridge or tunnel built to connect New Jersey and Manhattan. Builders, incorporators, civil engineers, and politicians got involved, but the conservative Pennsylvania decided to merely watch closely from the sidelines. In 1891 Congress approved a charter for the North River Bridge Company to build an unprecedented 150-foot high railroad suspension bridge over the Hudson, but the PRR remained cautious. By 1900 the PRR estimated they were carrying over 33 million people annually between New Jersey and Manhattan by ferry boats, and realized that they had to somehow link Manhattan and New Jersey by rail. Finally the

Pennsy got on the bandwagon and tried to interest the B&O, Lackawanna, Reading and Central of New Jersey in sharing the costs of a bridge. However these smaller railroads were satisfied with the ferries and would not take on part of the financial burden of the bridge.

During the last half of the decade of the 1890s the Pennsylvania had three different presidents: George Roberts, who died of a heart ailment in 1897, Frank Thomson, who succeeded Roberts but died just two and a half years later, and Alexander J. Cassatt, who succeeded Thomson in June 1899. Cassatt was determined to get the mighty Pennsylvania into Manhattan, just as arch rival New York Central was doing, and was interested in a tunnel to Staten Island, and thence Long Island, where the railroad would split with one bridge heading over the East River to Manhattan and the other line continuing north to reach the New Haven Railroad and a direct connection into New England. In the second quarter of 1900, the PRR secured 56.6% of the Long Island Rail Road's capital stock at a cost of $6.8 million, and the dream of having a direct link through Manhattan started to take shape. Like the railroads across the Hudson River in New Jersey, the Long Island was at a saturation point with its ferry boats trying to keep up with the escalating number of commuters. A quicker way of getting into Manhattan with greater capacity had to be found.

In December 1901 President Cassatt, mindful of the fact that the B&O was in its sixth year of electric operations through its Howard Street tunnel in Baltimore, announced to the public the Pennsylvania's decision to reach Manhattan via a series of tunnels that would accommodate safe, clean, quiet electric-powered trains, using all steel equipment. By December 1903 the railroad awarded contracts for a double track fill across the Hackensack Meadows, the Hudson tunnels from Bergen Hill, the Pennsylvania Station excavation and station design, a yard in Long Island City, the East River tunnels, and the track, signals, communications and electrical transmission system. In Altoona, the PK passenger car was virtually duplicated in steel, but proved to be a failure. The engineers went back to the drawing boards and came up with a new coach that held 72 people. Management said to build a larger car, so in 1907 the first fireproof P-70 was built. The Test Department set the car on fire to see if it really was fireproof and shortly thereafter the Railroad gave orders to car builders to start constructing steel P-70 coaches! By mid-summer 1904, work began on this most ambitious construction project ever taken on by any railroad. The actual development of motive power, the electric power generation system, and distribution has been covered in several books, reports, and magazines, and we'll touch upon some of it here in both pictures and captions.

Back at Penn Station, I try to contemplate how this magnificent palace fits into Pennsy's scheme of things from an historical standpoint. The Blue Ribbon fleet of trains has departed for the west, but there are people and trains coming and going, just as I had left it. In 1945, an unbelievable 190,000,000 people took trains in and out of here! Pennsylvania Station is the Railroad's public showcase, "A Trojan Horse right here on Manhattan Island, a massive insult to the Vanderbilts," as historian Nathaniel Burt once put it, shortly after it was built.

Walking through Penn Station, en route to the taxis, I imagined the incredible hatred that existed between the PRR and New York Central, knowing the Pennsylvania had started the massive undertaking to get into Manhattan before they even had suitable designs for electric-powered trains to go through the tunnels. I considered the Pennsy's known methodical approach to designing, building, and testing locomotive designs over periods of *years* before accepting motive power for service. The implication of developing power while the station project was underway is mindboggling.

Once over at Grand Central, I have a few minutes before the boarding begins for my local-express to Hartsdale. Since I have spent my life away from the Pennsy, I find myself making the inevitable comparisons. Penn Station has its Savarin, GCT has the Oyster Bar. GCT has the Roosevelt, the Art Gallery, the Biltmore, the Yale Club is next door, Brooks Brothers, Abercrombie & Fitch and Triplers are nearly as close. The New York Central dwells in the Vanderbilts' upper class Manhattan. Time to get on my train of somber Pullman green 4500 series streamlined MU cars for the quiet ride to Hartsdale. My fellow riders look like bankers, brokers, and lawyers as opposed to the blue-collar flavor of the Pennsy. With their

Times, Journals, and *Tribs* folded into neat half-page and quarter-page columns, they present a whole different picture from the *Daily News* and tabloid readers I was with on board the Pennsy. After today, the New York Central seems quite dull!

Memory is a force within all of us. I have immersed myself in Pennsy while writing this book, and many wonderful memories have come back to me.

During World War II, when I was about six years old, I made a trip from Kansas to New York with friends of my family. We traveled to St. Louis and then to Chicago, where we boarded a Pennsylvania train. The day was about as cheerless as one could ask for. Hordes of people rushed about, many of them soldiers who marched through the station or on the platform. The air was full of expectation—far more than befit the occasion. I could sense the restlessness of the people, anxieties amplified by signs of war everywhere, including the mural in Chicago Union Station depicting bombs falling on a green land covered with a Nazi swastika, and seemingly thousands of bombers hanging on wires from the ceiling. I still can recall the men in uniform, the people rushing about makeshift ticket windows, women trying to herd people through the station. Somehow there was organization in all of the chaos. My memories of the trip have long since faded, but other images, most distant and faint, are still present.

Nighttime to most of us is disquieting, eerie, unnatural, a time of stillness and silence. Any interruptions—a sudden bolt of lightning, a passing light—can be downright frightening. My memories of our train traveling through the night bring back fears similar to those of lightning at night. I mentioned before that the Pennsy was *different*. A green signal at night suddenly turning red in the wake of a train seems natural. But on Pennsy, the yellow eyes of position light signals out there in the dark always made me feel that creatures were glinting at us. Darkness outside the train is inextricably tangled with our own darknesses and inner fears and it is for this reason, I believe, my nocturnal memories of that train ride are so much more vivid than any others. (I will remember the occasional tower or station hidden in the dark grip of night, but in the daytime they are barely noticed and soon forgotten.)

Throughout the night torrents of trains passed us. I pressed my face against the window of the darkened coach and watched for the curves. Position light signals—cats' eyes, shining in the dark—at times dimmed by smoke, fog, or rain, were always there on the tangents, around curves, under bridges, before tunnels. These eyes haunted me in the black night. The rails would suddenly glow orange, then white from a headlight. In an instant, the slash of a white blade, windows, markers, darkness. Those cats' eyes always returned: *clear* ahead, *approach-medium* on the next track over.

We passed countless mills and factories that night—great, long, windowed buildings along the tracks. There were always engines and cars on sidings, usually silhouetted by the glare emitted from the various industries. At one point, we slowed to almost a crawl. Steam and smoke were rising in boiling torrents into a thick cloud bank over us. We were next to several buildings with many pipes going between them. I quickly caught a glimpse of a GI guard standing at the corner of one of the buildings. The light glinted on the steel of his bayonet. A steam locomotive roared past, blocking further view with its long passing train of hoppers. I felt our train starting to pick up speed and soon we were once again moving into the blackness.

At some point during the night after what could have been infinity—or only minutes, I woke up suddenly as we were passing a freight going our direction. This time, we were on the outside track and it was on our left, right next to me. Its cars were black shapes against a fiery red sky. We were overtaking it although neither one of us was moving that fast. Looking up, I saw the passing horizontal bars of the yellow-white position lights rimmed in smoke. Soon we leaned into a curve to the left, and as we overtook the freight, its headlight lit the side of our train and its two smoking engines. We overtook the freight's thundering engine and for an instant its crew and cab seemed ringed in flames. I could feel the locomotive's heat through my window and feel its thunderous stack. Its brilliant headlight lit up our car. The thousands of tons of passing steel seemed to set the stage for what was to come.

17

From the window I saw a fiery, fuming landscape: American industry was exploding with war production. Ugly, tormented shapes of imposing furnaces, stacks, ovens and towers illuminated the tracks. Overhead, flames licked the sky, haloed in smoke and gases. Inside some of the buildings the furious fires of the mills glowed; the roar and din of it all nearly drowned out the rumble of our train.

Everywhere I saw steel, white and steaming, against the backdrop of orange and red. I felt we were a little toy amidst this overwhelming holocaust. Cars and cars of black coal from inside the earth were everywhere to fuel the giant furnaces of war. Overhead cranes, conveyor belts, magnets and tongs, lifted, dumped, carried and poured tons of coal to fuel the furnaces. It seemed that America was at war on the homefront, and there I was, riding the Pennsylvania Railroad in the midst of it all! I was grateful for the sunrise.

Someone once asked Harold J. Ruttenberg, former director of the United Steelworkers of America and later president of Portsmouth Steel Corporation, "What is steel?" He immediately answered, "America!" Most of the years covered in this book are during the steel age, with Pittsburgh, the Gibraltar, where the Allegheny and the Monongahela join to form the Ohio. Pittsburgh got its start when small iron manufacturers sprang up in the nearby Pennsylvania hills, close to the coal mines. The railroads bought the iron rails and hauled the coal; in effect both mill and railroad building each other. After 1840, American iron started to be smelted with coke; and by the early 1860s, the Bessemer process of converting pig iron into steel using cold air under pressure in a converter was introduced and refined. On May 24, 1865, the first Bessemer steel rail was rolled in America. The Pennsylvania Railroad became the first railroad to change over from iron rail to steel and was the fledgling steel mill's biggest customer. Iron mogul, Andrew Carnegie, built the huge Edgar Thomson Works near Pittsburgh for the manufacture of rails, naming the plant after the president of his biggest customer, the PRR!

The Pennsylvania Railroad was incorporated by the Pennsylvania State Legislature on April 13, 1846, at a time when the Erie Canal, the New York & Erie Rail Road and Baltimore & Ohio were building westward. Reports from the time indicate there was great concern that the rivals would squeeze both Philadelphia and the Pennsylvania Railroad off the map if quick progress to build the railroad wasn't achieved. The one tremendous asset the PRR had that no one else had was the brilliant civil engineer, John Edgar Thomson. The original charter called for a railroad from Harrisburg to Pittsburgh, and while that segment was under construction, Thomson was thinking of ways of getting far beyond Pittsburgh. He also was working on taking over smaller strategic rail lines and even canal companies that would someday become key segments of the system. In 1856, two years before the first passenger train passed over the entire rail-route from Philadelphia to Pittsburgh, Thomson engineered a consolidation of small roads west of Pittsburgh into the Pittsburgh, Fort Wayne & Chicago Railroad which would later be leased, then bought, by the Pennsylvania. Thomson died in 1874, but the Railroad continued to expand under followers Thomas A. Scott, George B. Roberts, and Alexander Johnston Cassatt. Unlike most of the other railroads at the time, and notably the New York Central, the Pennsylvania was not a product of lawyers, financiers and society, but the result of bright civil engineers and capable construction crews.

By all reports, there was almost a fanaticism from day one to build and operate the Pennsy as a *railroad*. While moguls tinkered with their railroads for personal gain, enormous fortunes and social status, the men of the Pennsylvania strictly adhered to superior engineering, sound, conservative fiscal policy and the constant practice of improving the value and efficiency of property and rolling stock. Company policy was to recognize the most capable engineers and award them positions in top management. All of these builders had one goal in common—to build and make the Pennsylvania Railroad the finest railroad in the world. I once asked an executive of the Railroad what made the PRR so different from its competitors. He replied, "The Pennsy always stuck to its knitting."

Fortune Magazine talked about the Pennsylvania Railroad and what I call the almost paternal qualities that seem to be uniquely Pennsy. The writer cautioned: "*Do not* think of the Pennsylvania Railroad as a business enterprise. Think of it as a nation." The article went on to describe the Railroad's tremendous size, stating that "corporately it behaves like a nation . . . blankets the lives of its 100,000 citizens like a nation, requiring an allegiance as single as a patriot's." *Fortune* described the men who move the PRR's trains as "soldiers, subject to a strictly military discipline, orders, reprimands, citations, on call for duty day and night. There is only one satisfaction, a deep one common to the entire population [of PRR employees], and that is of performing the daily miracle of moving five thousand gigantic, temperamental, ponderous, menacing groupings of tonnage precariously from here to there."

Fortune likened the job of PRR's vice president in charge of operations to "the Secretary of War" under whose orders four regional vice presidents run the railroad through 28 division superintendents, who, in turn, issue orders through division engineers, trainmasters and master mechanics. At the top of the command, of course, is the president. His decisions quite clearly become system policy through orders, not arguments. The executives right under the president are there because they are the best, carrying on with the Pennsy's traditional way of doing things. When I once asked a middle-management level employee about what I perceived to be the PRR's irreverent disdain towards traditional railroading, he replied, "a lot of people accuse us of having a little incest. It's OK, since we only breed with our own kind."

Perhaps nowhere in the Railroad's broad policies of conservatism and efficiency was the manifestation of this thinking practiced more religiously than in the development and operation of its motive power. Starting in 1867, under the direction of John P. Laird, master of machinery, and Alexander J. Cassatt, superintendent of motive power and machinery, the Railroad's mechanical engineers began working up blue prints for eight new classes of locomotives that would be superior in their roles as switchers, freight and passenger engines; that would also allow for uniformity in plans and patterns and as many interchangeable parts as possible. By 1873, the Railroad had 873 locomotives on its roster out of which 373 were classed as "standard," although they represented ten different classes. To give this some meaning, the Railroad required a maximum of only four different patterns of brass or iron castings for any given part. Interchangeability was carried out to such a degree that forgings used for each class of locomotive were in most cases arranged into four basic groups. Each locomotive had approximately 245 forgings. The Railroad built most of these engines in their own Altoona Shops, and if any locomotives were built by commercial builders, everything was constructed to Company standards.

Shortly after the turn of the century, President Alexander Cassatt (a former motive power man) asked his chief of motive power, Theodore N. Ely, to work with his engineers and come up with a design for a complete facility to test and evaluate locomotives under various controlled operating conditions. What Cassatt asked for was something that no railroad or locomotive builder in this country had ever done. In 1904, the Railroad's Motive Power Department built their finished locomotive test plant at the Louisiana Purchase Exposition in St. Louis and actually tested eight different locomotives as part of the exposition. The complete plant was subsequently disassembled and rebuilt into a huge test department facility in Altoona. All new materials—everything!—that was going to be used on the Railroad was tested. Wheels, oily waste, locomotives, cars, coal, paint pigments, wood preservatives, lubricating packs, nonconductive electrician's gloves, everything! Why, the Test Department tested light bulbs—rows and rows of them—to see how bright each manufacturer's bulbs were, and how long they'd last. Brooms, you ask? The Pennsylvania Railroad Test Department's broom testing machine had all (or almost all) of the answers. Yes, there are some who say the PRR was a little excessive, a railroad where eccentricity was not only tolerated, but usually rewarded.

Without a doubt, the most intriguing story about the Pennsylvania is that of the general motive power development—and lack thereof—from the 1920s through the 1930s, followed by the sudden wartime need for new locomotives, and what appeared to be a mad rush to make up for lost time. I have elaborated on details and data pertaining to the individual classes in the photo caption-text, but an overall review is needed, too, beginning shortly after the turn of the century.

In 1914 eighty E6s class engines of the 4-4-2 wheel arrangement were being outshopped by Juniata. During the same year, the first K4s was completed in May at Juniata. Two years later, Juniata constructed the first I1s in an effort to improve upon the 574 class L1s Mikados built between 1914 and 1919. By 1924, a total of 598 of the big I1s were built, becoming the standard heavy freight engine on the PRR. Though lesser known among the ranks of Pennsy steam, all 109 of the N class 2-10-2s were outshopped in 1918 and 1919. From 1917 through 1928, all 424 production class K4s engines were completed. In the meantime, the road's newest locomotive, the prototype M1, rolled out of Juniata Shops in 1923. In 1926 and 1930 a total of 299 additional M class engines were built. Typical of the PRR's conservative practices, exhaustive road tests and test plant experiments were run on each prototype before production began. Conforming to Pennsy's unique standardized scheme of things, a quick glance at engine specs reveals the wide scale use of identical parts, from boilers to bolts. One of my favorite examples of Pennsy's thinking and one that profoundly illustrates company practice was when the Railroad realized in the early 1920s that it needed a new, standard locomotive for start-and-stop commuter service. Mechanical engineer, William F. Kiesel, Jr., took charge of the project and came up with the very successful G5s locomotive which rolled out of Juniata's erecting shop in 1923. While any other railroad would have ordered a 4-6-2, Kiesel's engine was a 4-6-0 which more than did the job, and with one less wheelset. A total of 369 hand-fired and 45 stoker-fired models were built. The G5s had that typical Pennsy look about her, and well she should, for her basic boiler was on 83 class E6 engines and over twelve hundred H8, H9 and H10 class engines! The standardization factor also enters into the unit cost figure, too. Each G5s and tender was outshopped for $35,590.

When we are talking about a railroad empire the size of the Pennsylvania, we are talking in terms of hundreds of locomotives in a single class, numbers that easily exceed total rosters on other class I railroads. And just as the Pennsy did not hesitate to build a horde of identical or standard locomotives it found to its liking, it also scrapped entire classes of locomotives that were no longer in favor with the motive power people. Between 1900 and 1945, over ten thousand locomotives became obsolete and were retired! Principal reasons for replacement were the heavier steel trains that required more power and better designs to allow for standardization and age. In 1851 the Railroad had 26 locomotives that had an average tractive effort of 5,287 pounds. By 1920 the roster had grown to 7,667 locomotives, each averaging 40,972 lbs. of tractive effort. By 1945, the total roster of locomotives was down to 4,718, but their average tractive effort was a hefty 58,673 lbs. That year 100 percent of the Railroad's available drawbar horsepower was split into 73 percent for steam freight power, 13.5 percent for steam passenger power, and about 6.7 percent for available steam switching power. The various classes of electric power accounted for the rest, and for much of the intrigue I find concerning Pennsy's motive power development.

On November 1, 1928 President William Atterbury formally announced that it was the Pennsylvania's intention to electrify the main line from New York to Wilmington, Delaware. The Railroad would also electrify the Low Grade Line from Philadelphia. Plans to build a large coal wharf at Thorndale were shelved. Atterbury stressed the greater savings using electricity in lieu of steam power, pointing out the increasing density of both freight and passenger business over the Railroad. Atterbury stressed that an electric locomotive must be designed to handle the increased size and weight of trains, operate at high speeds, and be totally reliable. He stated, "this electrification will exceed in magnitude and in importance that of any other railroad in the world." Public praise for the unprecedented proposal was great, but as could be expected, the National Coal Association bitterly criticized the Railroad for turning its back on coal and the steam locomotive. At the time of the announcement, the PRR was hauling 10 percent of the nation's coal and purchasing over 3 percent to burn in its locomotives.

The following year, the going for this expensive electrification project got tougher when the stock market crashed and money became tight. Pennsy's long-time electrical consultants, Gibbs and Hill, were retained to advise on everything from burying signal lines away from transmission and contact wires, to preparing the road bed and enlarging bridge and tunnel clearances for bigger and faster locomotives. Mechanical engineer, John Van Buren Duer was put in charge of the electrical engineering for the Railroad and was given the important title of chief electrical engineer, reporting directly to the operating vice president, John F. Deasy.

Steam men and mechanical engineers, Alfred W. Gibbs, Axel S. Vogt, and William F. Kiesel, Jr., were to work with Duer, primarily on electric locomotive design. Jackshaft electrics were considered, but their limitations were well known from the Railroad's own experience with them. In the late 1920s there was a major breakthrough in electric locomotive designs when a single-phase, a.c. commutator motor was designed to go between driving wheels. Three classes of box cab electrics were simultaneously ordered as experimental units: the O1 for light passenger train service, the P5 for heavy passenger work, and the L6 for heavy freight work. All three motors looked very similiar, and all three classes contained as many standard, interchangeable parts as possible. Eight O1 motors of slightly different designs were built and three of the L6 motors were built. The P5, hands down (or is that pans down!) was the runaway favorite.

In 1931, Altoona turned out the first two P5 electric locomotives which were the combined products of GE, Westinghouse, and the PRR. Every part and component was standardized in these locomotives to PRR specs. After undergoing testing, they were declared a great success. In an article prepared for *Electrical Engineering Magazine* in July 1932, Duer talked in terms of the new P5 taking over the K4s assignments on the New York Division: "Consideration was given to the horsepower and tractive effort of a steam locomotive that was handling through passenger trains successfully; it was felt that if an electric locomotive could be built with the same or better horsepower and tractive effort than that of this particular steam locomotive, the resulting electric locomotive would provide a satisfactory unit for handling through passenger trains." Ninety P5a motors followed between 1932 and 1935.

On February 17, 1931, after a meeting with the board of directors, President Atterbury announced that catenary would be continued to Washington and that more money would be spent on other electrification projects. The Railroad planned to finance the further electrification through earnings and the sale of bonds. Towards year's end, traffic had gone down to the point where officers' salaries had to be cut by 10 percent. On February 1, 1932 union employees agreed to take similar cuts. As traffic continued to decline, layoffs and deferred maintenance were instituted. It is said the Pennsylvania Railroad made as generous a contribution to the national deflation as any single corporation when it fired 67,000 men and cut its wage bill by $192,000,000 in the four years following 1929. Pennsylvania's annual report for 1931 proudly stressed that the Railroad was one of the few American railroads still operating in the black. After much persuasion, the Railroad got loans from the Reconstruction Finance Corporation (RFC), matched by loans from private sources. The electrification program continued. Electric train service between New York and New Brunswick began on December 9, 1932, followed by New York to Philadelphia electric service on January 16, 1933. On April 8, 1933, the *Broadway Limited* made its last run behind steam out of Manhattan Transfer, New Jersey.

By now, the Railroad realized that they were having some serious problems with the P5a motors in the form of high speed oscillation and cracks in the driving axles. The Railroad amassed its mechanical engineers and test department personnel to start work on designs for a replacement locomotive for the P5a, and at the same time thoroughly test the P5a to determine what could be done. A glorious sight to many, but an embarrassment to the brass was the return of the K4s under the wires in October 1933, as all of the motors were withdrawn from service for what the Company quietly and desperately hoped would be remedial modifications. Westinghouse and GE were asked to each come up with a locomotive more powerful than the P5a, with lighter axle loadings and the capability of handling 18 heavyweight cars at 100 miles per hour. After a grade crossing accident occurred in Deans, N.J. in January 1934, killing the engineer on board the recently returned to service P5a #4772, streamlined car bodies affording crew protection were stipulated for the new electric locomotive designs.

A special instrumented test track was set up at Claymont, Del., to measure stress forces on the rails at various speeds. Weigh bars and stress gauges were used on various P5 locomotives to measure lateral and vertical forces on axles and flanges, while oscillographs and other instruments were outfitted in a test car to measure stresses. It was during this period in late 1933 that the Railroad borrowed New Haven's EP-3 electric locomotive #0354 for testing at Claymont. She was built by General Electric in 1931, and unlike PRR's stout O1, P5 and L6 electrics that rode on fewer and much larger drive wheels, New Haven's motor gracefully rode on a twenty-wheel 2-C + C-2 wheel arrangement. She was regeared at the Wilmington shops for 120 mph and unlike the P5's almost 77,000 pounds per driving axle load, the EP-3 possessed twice as many drive axles with less than 46,000 pounds loading per axle. She was an elegant performer, running through the tests, showing off her superior tracking qualities. The Pennsy liked what they saw.

Trackside talk at Claymont and back in Altoona went along armature-in-armature (sorry!) with that of the Philadelphia brass that for once the Pennsylvania had gone ahead and built a locomotive (the P5) for service without taking the normal exhaustive steps of testing it. In a time of national economic distress, the electrification program was a triumph and it just outpaced any chances for the thorough development of a main line electric locomotive. With the Claymont tests largely behind, the Railroad was determined, P5 problems and all, not to rush with the tests of the two new prototype locomotives that were coming from Westinghouse and General Electric.

In an effort to concentrate the best genius of mechanical engineering talent on and into electrification, personnel changes that had begun a few years earlier accelerated. Altoona had not built a steam locomotive since M1a Mountain #6774 was outshopped in November 1930. The locomotive erecting shops had since been building mostly MP54 electric MU car bodies along with some L6, O1, P5a and B1 electrics. The floors were covered with neatly grouped traction motors, transformers, blowers, smoothing reactors, auxiliary electrical equipment, cab assemblies, etc.—not the trappings that were associated with steam.

The most noticeable personnel change that reflected the Railroad's obsession with electrification was naming John V. B. Duer chief electrical engineer reporting directly to Vice President Deasy. Another new job was that of electrical foreman, held by B. G. Gibson, whose job could also carry the title "chief trouble shooter." Good steam men like Carleton K. Stine, master mechanic, also found themselves working in the Wilmington Shops, far from the whistle of an I1. And almost on a weekly basis, more and more of his mechanical engineers traded their Altoona offices to become electrical engineers in Wilmington. The economy continued to slow and the Railroad was laying off more and more people. The scores of steam men who trained to run electrics held their jobs, but fewer mechanics (now, really electricians) were required to maintain the electric locomotives. The days when hundreds of standard steam locomotives were being assembled on Altoona's shop floors were now simply memories.

In August 1934, both the eagerly awaited R1 from Westinghouse and GG1 from General Electric were delivered to the PRR, arriving on the property together. Some PR photos were taken of each engine, but then it was off to Claymont for exhaustive tests. Sandhouse talk immediately started that the "Westinghouse job" was favored since it had the rigid frame in lieu of the jointed articulated frame, and consequently got the correct number (4800 for the R1 and 4899 for the GG1) to begin the series. For ten weeks, day-in, day-out, the R1 and GG1 ran hard and flawlessly. They matched each other through the test track and stayed with each other in regular service assignments. Both motors accelerated their trains in breathtaking fashion and even developed short-time ratings of over 10,000 horsepower. Only at speeds of 100 mph and higher did the GG1 go easier on the track. At the end of the trials, the GG1 won, the final verdict being that the R1's longer rigid wheelbase could be less safe on curves and turnouts. Also, the GG1's Type 627 traction motors were almost the same as the familiar ones already in use on the Company's MP54's. For the GG1, the victory was not only won this time, but for seasons and seasons to come. In my opinion, one of the test enginemen summed it up best when he offered that the "GG1 was like a blend of good sherry with some white lightning in it—smooth with a good strong finishing kick." On November 17, 1934 the Railroad ordered the first 57 production GG1s, retaining industrial designer, Raymond Loewy, to streamline the carbody. For the first time in years, men would be headed back to Altoona where GG1s would be taking over the erecting bays. The Railroad would quickly finish the last of the 28 P5a motors for which it had contracted in 1931, and all of the P5s would be regeared for freight service. Only one L6a class motor was completed in Lima out of an original order for thirty locomotives and the 29 additional carbodies for the L6a were sent to Hollidaysburg and eventually scrapped. Had the P5a worked out as a high speed passenger motor, the Railroad with its increasing war supply traffic would have been looking for a new freight locomotive, and, perhaps, with not enough time to test and perfect it! The first production GG1 arrived in April 1935. She was a sight to see—a testament of power at speed and a stunningly elegant machine at rest. The brunswick green and five gold pinstripes would be applied to all future electrics (and diesels) for the next two decades.

Let us not forget steam! While executives back in Philadelphia took pay cuts, dickered with the bureaucratic Reconstruction Finance Corporation for loans, jawboned with the Roosevelt Administration and bargained with the Public Works Administration for funding the electric construction, steam had seemingly disappeared from thought. While the Railroad dug two new tunnels and buried 132,000 volt transmission lines through Baltimore (against its wishes), and sought an act of Congress to string its a.c. catenary into the District of Columbia, steam had not been mentioned. While wires were strung west to Harrisburg over the Low Grade and Port Deposit Branch and over several freight yards, steam had yet to resurface. And while the new GG1s rolled onto their stage as *masters of the game*, the believers in steam knew that the GG1 had set new high standards for them to meet.

President Atterbury had retired in 1935 because of illness and was replaced by Martin W. Clement, who came up through the ranks with an engineering and operating background. Clement supervised the electrification under Atterbury and shared the dream of stringing wires as far as Pittsburgh, In 1936 Clement retained Gibbs and Hill to do a feasibility study on electrifying the Middle and Pittsburgh Divisions. This same year, the chief of motive power, Fred Hankins, and his whole group, including the Car Department and Locomotive Department moved from Altoona to Philadelphia. The Mechanical Engineers Department and Electrical Engineers Department also moved to Philadelphia. The Test Department and Works organization remained in Altoona. From Altoona west, many a PRR employee felt as though the brass had become blinded by electrification. Meanwhile, the extensive electrification study by Gibbs and Hill was completed in 1938. Among many things, the study recommended new GG1 type locomotives with larger transformers, a higher overall contact voltage, plus new tunnels through the Alleghenies to lessen the grade. The immediate costs were prohibitive, but the Executive Department authorized the design and construction of one 5000 horsepower prototype DD2 electric locomotive for freight and passenger use if . . .

Clement's top operating man, John F. Deasy, tried to spend two weeks of every month out on the Railroad. It was said that, like his boss, he knew every piece of the Railroad, and that he loved nothing more than a high speed ride down the main to Washington. Deasy was a believer in what he called his "axioms of railroad economics": Axiom 1. to load as much into every freight car as you can; 2. to put as many cars into one train as you can; and 3. to run as few trains as you can. On westward trips two K4s, two crews, and possibly two sections to handle the revenue did not set well with him. The Railroad, in effect, needed a steam-powered GG1 locomotive! It was rumored that Clement and Deasy, on rare occasions, drove just south of Philadelphia over to the Railroad in open country to "clear their minds" away from the office. Watching a GG1 appearing as a distant speck behind a yellow headlight, then pass by seconds later like silent lightning propelled with the furious force of electricity, was enough to convince them that they had a hell of a railroad—back East. They needed this same kind of operation on the western end across Ohio and Indiana.

Late in 1937 President Clement convened a meeting with representatives of Baldwin, American Locomotive and Lima to discuss the prospect for a steam locomotive that would do what a GG1 could do, namely, haul 1200 tons at 100 miles per hour. Fred Hankins, Pennsy's CMO, along with H. W. Jones and Carleton Stine, represented the nucleus of mechanical engineering talent for the PRR. There was no worry of anti-trust in those days, and it was the Railroad's desire to assemble the best talent possible to try to come up with *the* passenger steam locomotive. A committee was formed with members representing the PRR and the three commercial builders. Preliminary design work began on paper immediately. Back in 1932 Baldwin advocated a duplex design steam locomotive using two sets of cylinders to lighten machinery weight and reduce pounding, as well as handle steam more efficiently. The Railroad still believed in this design. In 1938 two events occurred that had a profound effect on the design of the new engine: First, Chicago & North Western's gargantuan 84″ drivered super Hudson #4003 was tested on the railroad and on the test track in the locomotive test plant and secondly, the Franklin poppet valve system was tested on K4s #5399. The big E-4 Hudson proved that 84″ drivers exerting 55,000 pounds of tractive effort need not be slippery and the poppet valve K4s showed a remarkable 24.2 percent increase in drawbar horsepower over a standard K4s at 60 miles per hour and an incredible 44 percent increase at 80 miles per hour, developing 4300 indicated horsepower instead of the normal 3500 horsepower for a K4s. The coal-hauling, coal-minded Pennsy was jubilant over the prospects of coming up with their own *super* steam locomotive!

Altoona, Eddystone, Lima and Schenectady's never before dreamed of giant 6-4-4-6 duplex started to take shape on the drafting boards at Baldwin with Altoona carrying out the engineering to the construction phase. When the new engine's 97,400 pound, 77 foot, 9½-inch long, Commonwealth cast steel engine bed arrived, the size of this giant was fully appreciated. Gone were the days of standardization, but certainly not the customary non-comformity. The incredible 140-foot, 84″ drivered 1 million pound monster was completed in January 1939, dwarfing the surrounding GG1s in the erecting bays. Before going to work on the Railroad, the "big engine" (as employees called her) went to the New York World's Fair where she churned away on rollers for two years, thrilling crowds. Once back on the Railroad, the huge Goliath ran as fast as any GG1 on her race track between Crestline and Chicago. She was slippery at times, but her only real problem was that she was just too big and powerful for the job she was designed for, and that's a real tribute to the genius of reciprocating steam power. Once again, in 1941, the Clement administration asked Gibbs and Hill to look at electrification costs for the existing Middle and Pittsburgh Divisions without any of the major line changes that the 1938 report advocated. This time, however, the Railroad couldn't continue with any serious work on electrification, as other things were happening in the world—and to Pennsy's traffic—that were beyond the Railroad's control.

In early October 1941 the Germans were advancing closer and closer to Moscow in their relentless drive across the Soviet Union. The destruction of great cities, the vanishing of ancient nations, the massive death struggle of armies, was an old story to many Americans so that the peril of Moscow hardly seemed real. Moscow was just another city on a timetable: Vienna, Prague, Warsaw, Copenhagen, Oslo, Rotterdam, Brussels, Sedan, Paris, Belgrade, Athens, Minsk, Kiev. And now, perhaps Moscow. Americans knew that if Russia fell, we would be left totally alone in the world with only Britain at our side.

An increasingly uneasy America faced two oceans filled with peril. In Japan, civilian premier Prince Tumimaro Konoye yielded his beleaguered government to the belligerent Lt. General Hideki Tojo, who was considered a friend of the Axis and a trigger-happy warmonger. The largest air raid defense drills ever staged in the U.S. commenced on Monday, October

20, along the mid-Atlantic seaboard, lasting throughout the entire week. American bombers were used, winging their way in off the Atlantic with interceptors scrambling, based on actual sightings by over 1600 observation posts, coordinated through the New York Information Center. In Washington, the reports coming over the radio concerned arming our merchant ships and dispensing with the Neutrality Act. Many of the staunch isolationist blocks, it seemed, were starting to break up. More and more, editorials, public figures and advertisements were urging America to get ready to fight.

October 28, 1941 is one of those clear, shimmering days, unusual for a normally dreary, normally smoky Altoona. The temperature at the Railroad Test Department building was 42 degrees at 9:00AM and it must be over 50 degrees now. By afternoon, it's supposed to be around 60 degrees in the Mountain City and throughout the Logan Valley. Last night, the PRR shop men and their families from the Altoona Works Local No. 42 of the Brotherhood of Railroad Shop Crafts of America met at the Jaffa Mosque and went on record opposing any increase in milk above 13 cents a quart. There was not any formal talk of war preparations, just mention of one of our destroyers being hit by a German torpedo and the Nazis nearing Moscow. Today's unseasonable weather makes it a day to be outside as much as possible. Tomorrow's forecast calls for much colder weather. By this evening, the warm weather will have gone, and the theatres in town will have little trouble tempting customers to come inside and enjoy a movie. At the Olympic they're showing *Parachute Battalion* with Robert Preston, Nancy Kelly, and Harry Carey. And at the Capitol is *Hold Back the Dawn.*

Down through *Alto's* interlocking, heading eastward, is a long train of coal-stained hoppers clanking and clattering, its noise resounding under the 17th Street Bridge. Even the rattling of the Altoona & Logan Valley 140-series Brill trolley, going over the bridge, is subdued by the heavy inbound coal train's racket. Some men come out of the front door of the red brick Test Department building and gather up on the bridge overlooking the tracks. They are some of the two hundred or more PRR employees of the "TD" whose dedicated talents, research, tests, and toil have resulted in locomotive creations that have roared all over Pennsy's rails—some to ultimate sucess, some to dismal failure. One holds today's *Altoona Mirror.* "John L. Lewis," he snarls. "That damn bastard doesn't care what he does." He holds up the headline for his coworkers to see: "Nation to Combat Strike menace."

Dusty Rhodes nods his head eastward. "He's not out yet," he says.

"Is Al Girtz on the engine?" Carl Nordberg asks. "Is Mr. Barrett with him?"

Dusty just shakes his head. "Don't know," he mutters; "Girtz should be onboard."

Men are now leaning out of the Test Department windows, hollering to the guys on the bridge. "Who of our guys is on board?" someone yells.

"Bob Pilcher and Ken Foley's on the engine and Pinky Blair's back in the car out of Roanoke," someone answers. "But I haven't heard about our guys. Oh yeah, Al Thompson is on the engine!"

More and more men gather on the bridge, joined by other people coming out of the Test Department building. There is a tense feeling in the air as the men peer eastward toward the 12th Street pedestrian bridge and beyond toward East Altoona. Across the tracks, shoppers heading into Wolf's Furniture Store seem to sense the excitement and pause to look up at the crowd on the bridge. The railroad *is* Altoona, and outsiders have learned to live with it rather than get involved in it.

Finally—"There, listen." Off to the east is a distant, thunderous *rah, rah, rah,* noticeably louder than the customary sound a train makes moving out of Altoona. The steady, pulsing, gunning roar echoes around the town and through the shops. A pillar of steam can now be clearly seen, etched against the clear, blue sky. Closer and louder, the spectacle comes. A few more guys from the Test Department move out to the bridge. The white plume turns gray and is menacingly large in shape, boiling up into the sky. Down the tracks an incredible blast of steam shoots out from under and around the 9th Street footbridge, followed by the blast under the 12th Street bridge. The approaching engine is now clearly seen, and it is clearly different from anything the Pennsy has run through town. A low pilot-mounted headlight leads the huge machine up the tracks, followed by double cylinders

25

under a long boiler. The pounding exhaust is excruciatingly sharp, like the crack of a rapid-fire twelve-gauge shotgun going off next to you in damp woods. Ears are covered as the huge articulated blasts past with a tremendous outpouring of raw power and its fascinating array of synchronized machinery. Number 1208 is on the cab with NORFOLK AND WESTERN spelled out along her tender. Norfolk and Western's maroon dynamometer car 514780 is almost lost in the smoke and steam coming out from under the bridge, but she is on the train and that is what some of the guys also wanted to see. The noisy engine whams its powerful exhaust at the 24th Street bridge and passes out of sight, leaving skeins of steam hanging in the air. Over the sounds of the rumbling freight cars, the thunderous cadence of the class A returns, seemingly echoing from all over the city. Most everyone stays around on the bridge and watches the passing train. Two I1sa Decapods approach on the rear end, kicking up a fuss, raising smoke and steam. But somehow, it is nothing like the A's. Maybe it's just familiarity. The Test Department guys doff their hats to the tried, true and familiar heading west behind the train. The I1s represent the men's own pasts as well as the Railroad's. The ghostly owl-hoot of the 1208's whistle comes back to us from the brick yard crossing, a whistle quite unlike anything ever heard around here.

In keeping with Railroad practice, nothing much was said about the Norfolk and Western engine. She lost a bolt on her reverse lever that day, halting progress until a temporary quick-fix remedy could be made with a cotter pin. They tied up in Crestline overnight and took general merchandise across the Ft. Wayne Division the next day. Not many people heard why the engine was on the property, although the Test Department later learned that the three biggest problems on the run with the engine were excessive back pressure, high water consumption and a tendency for the lead engine to slip. Poor coal was suspected. One other annoyance was the fact the N&W engine didn't have a water scoop and consequently tied up the main line each time it needed water.

Shortly after the Norfolk and Western A had completed tests on the Pennsylvania, America's war preparations reached a more urgent pace. John L. Lewis's six day coal-mine strike was not the intended show of unity, but rather pitted strikers against patriots who felt they should work for the defense of our country. At the big C.I.O. convention in Detroit on November 17, John L. Lewis was repudiated. But what really brought home the prospect of war did not come from Washington, nor from FDR's addresses, nor from patriotic campaigns. It came from brilliantly executed maneuvers between our Army, Navy, Marines and Air Corps off the Atlantic Coast, in the Caribbean and in the Pacific. Closer to home, the Army Air Corps had built countless "hidden airfields" simulating European conditions and had been coordinating with ground maneuvers using bombs and live ammunition over and on American soil. Bombers had started flying out of muddy fields, making low level bomb runs along rivers and over fields. Major General Herbert Dargue of the First Air Force said that "the Army and the Air Force are learning to get in the mud and wallow together." In North Carolina attack bombers had been raking practice areas with machine gun fire and fragmentary bombs, followed by C-47s and parachutists and color-coded chutes with TNT for demolition, mortars, tommy guns and machine guns. As B-17 and B-24 bombers practiced bomb runs with their huge 1100 and 2000-pound bombs off the Atlantic Coast, new pursuit tactics with new planes were happening in the skies throughout the country. Newspapers and newsreels featured Americans getting ready for war on a daily basis— getting ready on and over American soil.

The PRR was now really in the crunch of wartime traffic; the brunt of which was being handled by three hundred and one 4-8-2s and five hundred and ninety-eight 2-10-0s. The newest group of steam locomotives on the system were one hundred of the 4-8-2s, now twelve years old. After the success of the 6-4-4-6 duplex #6100, the road ordered two experimental 4-4-4-4 passenger duplex locomotives from Baldwin and one experimental 4-6-4-4 freight duplex from Altoona, all three locomotives were slated for second quarter 1942 delivery. Just a month after the Norfolk and Western's articulated locomotive completed its tests on the PRR, Chesapeake & Ohio's powerful, drag-loving Texas type #3015 arrived on the property for a briefer schedule of tests. Pennsy's dynamometer car

495591 was still in the car shops being rebuilt into a steel car so it was not available for any tests with the C&O engine.

Word came from Philadelphia that, unlike all of the testing done on the N&W engine, the C&O locomotive would be put to work on the Railroad and would be the responsibility of Al Girtz, chief coal inspector, who reported to R. G. "Bobby" Bennett, assistant chief mechanical officer–locomotives. "Smoke" Suhrie would be the trouble shooter (special duty engineman) reporting directly to Bennett. The standard practice of having either the road foreman or his representatives in the cab would be followed on every division the 3015 operated on and in all cases, a regular crew would be called.

The first run for the big Lima-built 2-10-4 was from East Altoona to Conemaugh on a hopper train. Engine reports right from the first run concurred that she was about the "fastest stepper out of Altoona" that anyone had yet seen on tonnage. She stood 16'7" tall over the stack, had huge 29" × 34" cylinders, an enormous 162" × 108¼" firebox, a tremendous 108" diameter boiler and could throw 108,625 pounds of tractive effort down on the rails. The T-1 really gained favor once it was realized that she took far less turn-around time at the end of a run than the Railroad was used to. As to be expected, a lot of sandhouse talk emanated from her cab, most notably from C&O's traveling engineer, Homer Fuller, (not the Homer Fuller of PRR) who related how a T-1 could take her 160-car, 13,500-ton coal train and out accelerate an N&W class A on similar tonnage, heading out of South Columbus on the parallel track. Regardless, the 3015 was the essence of Lima's high-horsepower, super power, and what impressed Pennsy is the fact that although the T-1's tractive effort was only slightly more than an I1sa, the horsepower output was just about double. And considering the fact that the Pennsy was basically a fifty miles per hour freight railroad, the A's reputed speed was not a decided advantage over the C&O T-1. Finally, the nonarticulated C&O engine was more to Pennsy's way of thinking.

No doubt about it, the PRR had tested two of the finest modern steam locomotives in America, and an entire book could be devoted to the tests and an ensuing debate on each class. The Pennsylvania was in a stressful period when the railroad was being hurt by the surge of tonnage and they needed a new freight engine badly. The maintenance of way people were very persuasive in their argument for divided drive locomotives to lighten reciprocating machinery and lessen destruction of the rail and roadbed, so the divided drive of the A was very desirable. Indeed, while both of the engines were running on the Railroad, Lima Locomotive Works was outshopping their order No. 1154 for ten huge 2-6-6-6 articulateds for the C&O to in effect replace the mighty T-1s. The Pennsylvania asked for photos and specs on this new H-8 locomotive, but arrangements could not be made to test it. The ten engines had more power than the T-1s, plus a decided advantage in speed. The Railroad was under pressure to come up with a suitable locomotive fast, and the thought of going with an articulated scared them on two counts: one was the immense size, machinery-wise, and the amount of time it would take to assemble a fleet of them. The other, and perhaps more understandable reason, was the tendency for the A to be a little slippery in the lead engine on less then ideal track conditions, such as on a sag, or on wet, greasy rails. The T-1 could spread her 373,000 pound tractive weight on her 10-coupled drivers, giving her undivided attention (couldn't resist that one) to producing its high 4.00 factor of adhesion. The A, on the other hand, with virtually the same factor of adhesion, pulling 33" above the rail, could unload several thousand pounds of weight off the front end of the locomotive on uneven rail, making her slippery. The A was a Cadillac capable of moving 14,000 tons at 70 miles per hour over level rail on the N&W. The fact that the 1208 developed high back pressure, using up too much water too quickly during the fast running over the Ft. Wayne Division remains a mystery for a class A is tops as an efficient, high-capacity, free-steaming locomotive. Al Girtz and Bob Stettler reported a great deal of trouble shaking the grates while #1208's fire was cleaned in Ft. Wayne. One can only speculate that, unlike the N&W where the best coal and treated water are used in their locomotives—which are operated to a science—maybe conditions on the PRR were just not digestable for the A.

The Pennsylvania took into account that the general freight limit was 50 miles per hour and that they needed a locomotive with the proven ability to dig in on the east and west slopes. They were aware of the fact that the N&W operated the As on the moderate to flat profiles on their railroad, while the C&O T-1s routinely lugged northbound coal upgrade out of Kentucky on the run to Russell. Once underway, the T-1 could do a decent 60, fast enough—really, too fast—for open-top loads in Pennsy's way of thinking.

Paperwork was exchanged between the C&O and PRR, red tape with the War Production Board cut through, and all material and suppliers quickly lined up. One hundred and twenty-five J1 engines were ordered in early March 1942, with Altoona outshopping the first completed engines in December of the year. In the rush of exchanging information and prints with the C&O, the original 1928 Lima prints were used for Altoona's construction, and it was only discovered that the latest up-to-date prints were not sent *after* the first J1s were completed. Needless to say, most of the 100 modifications that C&O made had to be subsequently done on the PRR engines. The biggest problem was counter-balancing the behemoths. Charles D. Barrett, assistant engineer of tests, and Eddie Girtz supervisor of the dynamometer car, took the first J out on the Pittsburgh Division to check on destructive effects from piston thrust at 45 to 50 miles per hour; nothing happened. Westward out of Columbus, Al Girtz put on the dynamometer car and Charlie Barrett rode the cab looking for suitable down-grade tangents where he could drop off the engine and watch from the ground. "Go back and bring her down at 70 or 75!" became a familiar order to the crew. To the chagrin of the maintenance of way department, plenty of track toward Indianapolis was kinked! Carleton Stine from the mechanical engineer's office in Philadelphia set up a program in the Columbus shop to make the necessary changes to the J1s, including counterbalancing. Work was also set up at the Altoona E&M shop (Erecting and Machine), the only other facility on the system equipped with 250-ton traveling overhead cranes required for the modifications.

In what I can describe only as Pennsy's cussedly determined attitude to be different, the Railroad outshopped their Q1 duplex 4-6-4-4 freight experimental in May 1942. She had ungainly high 77″ drivers, a grate area of a mere 98.3 square feet and a tractive effort of 81,793 pounds without booster. Her rear cylinders faced forward, limiting firebox size and accessible maintenance while, at the same time, collecting dirt. Perhaps, her crowning achievement was that of revealing her "1,000,000 pound club membership status" at a display at the south end of Thirtieth Street Station on the lower level shortly after she was built. She spent the rest of the war unloved and unwanted in service between shoppings west of Pittsburgh. Passenger hauling T1 locomotives #6110 and 6111, delivered in 1942 fared much better during the war years, blazing across the flats of Ohio and Indiana lobbying relentlessly for the duplex design, as well as replacements for double-headed K4s class engines. The T1s were slippery, but received spectacular praise for their service. In 1946, a fleet of fifty more of the rakish 4-4-4-4 duplexes were ordered. While the Second World War raged on, men like Carleton Stine, Harry Decker and H. W. Jones spear-headed design work and construction of the ultimate duplex drive freight locomotive for the Pennsylvania Railroad, the Q2. The attraction of the duplex was the divided drive which permitted lower dynamic augment because of the lighter weight machinery. The first 4-4-6-4 class Q2 was completed at Altoona in August 1944, and was immediately placed in service on the Railroad. She was a titanic ground shaker and produced close to 8000 ihp (indicated horsepower) under controlled tests. She and her 25 production sisters may have achieved *the* highest power output for any steam locomotive. The Pennsy loved 'em and cancelled an order that was placed with Lima for twenty-five more 2-10-4s.

But let's take a quick look at the J1 and Q2 engines together. The J1 had only about 200 square feet less heating surface than the Q2. Both engines had equal sized grate areas and 69″ drivers. The J1 had about 5700 pounds less cylinder tractive effort. On controlled tests, the J1 produced about 7000 ihp at 57 miles per hour with a 56 percent cutoff (compared to the Q's 8000 ihp with a 40 percent cutoff). In the railroad's 50 miles per hour service, these differences would be minimal, the major advantage going to the Q2's lighter reciprocating parts and better proportioned steam passages. Things get interesting, however, when you realize the Q2 is, in effect, paying a dead weight penalty of 43,220 pounds for 1000 more indicated horsepower at 57 miles per hour. The Qs ran at 30 psi more than the J1 and had Belpaire boilers. Comparing piston thrusts between the two (the full boiler steam pressure acting on the surface area of the piston), the J1's thrust was a hefty 178,300 pounds for each cylinder, while the Q2's piston thrusts were a modest 92,000 and 133,000 pounds respectively for the front and rear cylinders. At the railroad's posted freight speed of 50 miles per hour, however, the possible destructive characteristics of the J1 were almost non-existent. The Q2s did not know how to conserve water and in short time enginemen were told to plan "no more than an hour and a half of hard running before needing water." Cost-conscious Pennsy soon found the duplexes also had a habit of spending more time in the shops than originally planned and started to weigh the in-service performance against out-of-service time. When all of the Q2s developed leaks in the barrel seam of the boilers just ahead and back of the second set of cylinders, extensive work was required to do the caulking of the boilers. This work was divided up between the Canton Enginehouse, Columbus Shop and the Altoona Works. A story went around the Railroad that Jack Francis, master mechanic at Conway, got on the phone one day with Chief Mechanical Officer H. T. Cover in Philadelphia frantically screaming that he had twenty-five Q2s out of service!

With the ensuing problems that developed with the Q2s and the increasing time they spent in shops, many of the M1s went back into service on the Fort Wayne Division and for a while, the standard machines of Wallis, Kiesel, Gibbs, and Vogt were showing folks what standard railroading should be like. The newer J1s were placed in heavy coal service on the Pittsburgh Division and were not wanted by enginemen on the Fort Wayne racetrack to pinch hit for the out-of-service Q2s. When a J1 *did* show up, however, enginemen soon discovered the properly counter-balanced engines could run like deer!

One month after the great Q2 duplex #6131 was completed at Altoona, perhaps the most exotic attempt ever at preserving steam locomotion emerged from the erecting shop at Baldwin in the form of Pennsylvania's class S2 steam turbine #6200. The handsome 6-8-6 mammoth was a no-nonsense straightforward machine that looked like a conventional steam locomotive at first glance, but a closer look revealed the absence of cylinders, pistons and valve gear. The boiler was a conventional fire-tube type with a 310 psi working pressure. Separate turbines for forward and reverse motion were mounted on the bed casting between the second and third pair of driving wheels which they drove through connected double-reduction gearing. The engineer merely had to open one lever for steam to shoot against the turbine blades which then drove the roller-bearing side rod connected driving wheels. "The simplest locomotive of any kind in the U.S.," Pennsy boasted.

Baldwin's pitch was that if the railroads were willing to pay twice the price of a modern conventional steam locomotive for a diesel electric, then they would welcome the advantages of a coal burning turbine that cost less than the comparable diesels yet would out perform them at all speeds above forty miles an hour. The question from the beginning was whether the steam turbine's simplicity and smoothness, top performance and low steam consumption at high speed, and reduction of dynamic augment would outweigh the maintenance on the turbine blades and gears, as well as the inefficient use of steam at slower (starting) speeds.

The machine went to work on the Fort Wayne Division and handled a range of assignments from general merchandise to the crack *Broadway Limited*. After several thousand miles of road service, the S2 went east to Altoona for inspection and stationary tests, where she developed 7245 horsepower at the turbine shaft at 66 miles per hour. The turbine blades showed only slight erosion and the geared transmission was in almost like new condition. The big strike against the locomotive was its high steam demand at low speeds and consequent related extremes in pressure and temperatures on the boiler. The Railroad was sufficiently impressed with the steam turbine to announce on March 20, 1944 that it would build a 9000 horsepower "triplex" turbine machine to be designed by

Westinghouse and built in Altoona. The engine would have two turbines geared to diesel-sized drive wheels under a forward coal bunker and under the firebox-first boiler. After the initial announcement, not much was said about the project. Speculation was that the Railroad retreated to a wait-and-see attitude to watch what the other railroads were doing with plans for coal-fired locomotives, and perhaps see how the diesels were doing.

In December 1944 the Pennsylvania borrowed Norfolk and Western's 70″ drivered streamlined J class 4-8-4 #610 for tests on the Fort Wayne Division. This locomotive represented the state-of-the-builder's-art in modern reciprocating steam locomotives for passenger service. All reports stated that the roller-bearing, high-powered engine quickly reached peak horsepower around 40 miles an hour, handling 1200 ton passenger trains at ease over the division, and knocking off 100 miles per hour, where conditions permitted. Once again, as was the case with the C&O and its T-1, the N&W furnished the wrong drawings showing J class engines 600–605 with the multiple bearing type crossheads. The 606 through the 610 had the larger alligator crossheads—a fact which was discovered when the 610 arrived at Chicago Union Station on Track 30, knocking off part of the concrete platform in the process! An embarrassed N&W quickly furnished the proper clearance diagram for the 606–610 class engines!

The Pennsy liked the N&W 4-8-4s, but seemed more preoccupied with the S2 turbine, the two in-service T1s, the new Q2s and, I suspect, the EMD diesels that were dashing around over other railroads. EMD's onslaught of diesels right after the war was accompanied by beautifully slick promotional campaigns, an incredibly effective sales engineer force, and attractive financing. Logic would dictate that Philadelphia was keeping a sharp eye on all of this. We have to remember the PRR's admiration for electric traction, and the fact that the diesel locomotive simply was, in effect, a portable power plant and generator supplying electricity to its traction motors, without the expense of catenary and power-distribution.

Right after the war, much talk ensued on our coal reserves. The fact that the 3.2 trillion tons of coal beneath the continental U.S. was close to half the world's known supply. Coal, however, was looked upon as a laggard—economically, socially, and technically. An article in *Fortune* magazine stated that "not only is our mining of coal inefficient, but we transport it in uneconomical fashion and consume it insensibly." A *Fortune* editorial stressed also that "something must be done about the miseries of coal."

In 1945, two right-off-the-shelf EMD model E7 diesels were delivered to the Pennsylvania Railroad. Lloyd M. Morris, assistant engineer of tests rode the two experimental units on their first run and "didn't think much of 'em." They were placed in pool service between Baltimore, Harrisburg and Detroit and then assigned to Nos. 68 and 69 between Harrisburg and Detroit. Nothing much was said about them although they were moved into more important assignments between Harrisburg and St. Louis in August 1946. The following June, both units were reassigned to the premier Harrisburg-to-Chicago service where management wanted to see what they could really do. Following Company policy, not much was said: putting diesels to work on a railroad that derived so much revenue from hauling coal seemed outright repugnant, if not suicidal.

When the Pittsburgh Consolidation Coal Company announced March 25, 1947 that they were going to build a $300,000 pilot plant to process coal into gas and diesel oil by 1950–51, the news was received with widespread enthusiasm by the PRR. The *Pittsburgh Press* called the announcement the "Biggest story in the history of coal." The Pennsylvania Railroad was buoyed to continue the design and engineering of coal-fired locomotives. Although 95 percent of all new locomotives on order in the U.S. at the time of Pitt Consol's announcement were diesels, representatives of the M.A. Hanna Co., Island Creek Coal, Sinclair Coal, Pocahontas Fuel and eight railroads, including the Pennsylvania, were working on a new coal-burning locomotive that utilized a combustion turbine and eight traction motors, gear connected to the axles. Suppliers included Allis-Chalmers and the Elliot Co. of Jeannette, Pa. for the turbines, and American Locomotive and Baldwin Locomotive for the chassis and running gear. A release said the new locomotive would be "The first effective challenge that coal has given oil in the twentieth century." Once again, however, this latest project to counter the diesel died away.

In February 1947 the Pennsylvania handled the movement of six modern 4-6-6-4 Challengers from East St. Louis to Hawthorne (Indianapolis) and on into the St. Clair yard in Columbus for interchange with the N&W. These engines were built by Alco in 1943 for the Union Pacific, but were diverted by the War Production Board on a lease basis to the traffic-clogged Denver & Rio Grande Western to supplement their own Baldwin-built class L-105 Challengers. After the war, the War Assets Administration sold them to the Clinchfield Railroad and consequently they appeared en route to the CRR on the Pennsy. A few years earlier—maybe even a year earlier—the PRR would most likely have taken a real close look at these modern steamers, and might have possibly tested one in Altoona. The absense of any comment about these engines said plenty about the Railroad's emerging policy on motive power. The six huge 4-6-6-4s were merely placed on scheduled freights to work their way east. Enginemen were told not to handle them over the posted speed limit of fifty miles per hour. The only hitch was that their big 14-wheel centipede tenders were too high for Pennsy's water plugs. Since the water hatch collars were 14 feet, $8\frac{5}{16}$ inches over the top of the rail, the Rose Lake shop forces had to cut holes in the back of the 25,000 gallon tenders and weld crude boxlike gutters to enable taking on water from the plugs. Needless to say, this arrangement presented quite a challenge to enginemen when they spotted the tenders at plugs!

At the same time the Clinchfield engines were on the property, eight more sets of A-B-A passenger E7 diesels were ordered from EMD for the Harrisburg-to-St. Louis service. During this same period, the Railroad turned to Alco, Baldwin, and Fairbanks-Morse, orders in hand, for more passenger diesels. By the end of 1947, the Railroad had a whopping 358 diesel locomotives in service, or on firm order.

In 1947 and 1948, neighbor Chesapeake & Ohio ordered 105 steam locomotives, from 0-8-0s to giant 2-6-6-6s while Norfolk and Western started building thirty more 2-8-8-2 mallets of the Y6b designation. The N&W also committed funds for building eight new class A locomotives, three class J engines, and forty-five more S1 class 0-8-0s. On the PRR, the story was much different. In the first three quarters of 1947, the Pennsylvania lost over 7 million dollars, but in the same period for 1948, it earned a respectable $17,600,000— enough to talk about new designs for an electric freight locomotive, and to justify more orders for diesel locomotives.

In March 1948, arrangements were initiated out of Philadelphia for the Norfolk & Western to borrow and test a T1 locomotive. The official word from the PRR was that President Clement thought the N&W "might be interested in the experimental use of the T1 passenger locomotive to compare it with one of their own J class engines." Pennsy operating officials, accountants, roundhouse foremen and engine crews had their own versions of what was behind the tests. In May of 1948 the Pennsylvania suggested the N&W might also want to test a class Q2 locomotive to see how it compared with an N&W class A. Some of the test results are compiled at the end of this text.

By the end of 1948, 352 diesels were on the property with 238 more on order. The great T1s occasionally roared across the Fort Wayne Division, but they were now shadows crossing the stage like the ghosts in *Macbeth*.

By 1949 there was no longer pretext on the part of the Pennsylvania Railroad involving their commitment to convert from coal to internal combustion locomotives. Men like Bill Porter, master mechanic at Columbus, started to sneak promising young special apprentices and management trainees off of the steamers and onto the diesels out at Nelson Road and at the St. Clair Avenue enginehouse, where "there was a future for the guys." Down on the C&O, thirty of the brand new 0-8-0s hardly had their grates warm when the railroad dropped the fires and sold them to the N&W in 1949. The three monstrous C&O steam turbines that were built in late 1947 were placed in storage in 1949, the same year repair work on Pennsy's steam turbine #6200 was stopped at Crestline. It was also in 1949 that the Gulf Mobile & Ohio Railroad dieselized, thus becoming the nation's first major railroad to completely drop steam from its locomotive roster. Among the GM&O's much publicized claims was that their 235 new diesels would do the work of 336 steam locomotives, with the average monthly mileage for the diesels reaching 10,000 miles in lieu of the 4,000 mile figure for steam. The wire services reported that when the last scheduled steam run was dieselized, the engineer climbed down from his clean new cab at the end of the run and said "Lord, God, this is white collar!"

Pennsy management kept a close watch on what rival New York Central was doing with its motive power, and specifically with the diesels. Of special interest to the PRR in the postwar years was Central's Boston & Albany line and its mountainous profile through the Berkshires. If any piece of railroad on the Central offered operating conditions similar to what the Pennsy had to contend with in the Alleghenies, it was the B&A. In 1947 diesels appeared on the Boston & Albany to work the line on a trial basis; in 1948 more diesels arrived *en masse* to tangle with the mountains, and with the steamers. The new engines surpassed all expectations in performance and operating costs and in a little over a year, by 1949, all steam was removed from the B&A rails so that the diesels could take over.

By year's end 1949 the Pennsylvania Railroad Company had spent 170 million dollars for just under 600 diesels, plus the maintenance and repair facilities to support them. Most of the Q2s were removed from service and stored at Crestline to rust away, while the fleet and gallant T1s were ending up their once promising careers on mail and express trains. Ironically, while the Railroad was ignoring the diesel's great potential for standardization by ordering a bit of everything from all of the diesel builders, they were turning back to the standard off-the-Altoona-shelf steam locomotives to close out the last decade of steam service on the Railroad. With the exception of the C&O/Lima-inspired J1s, the distinction of closing out 111 years of steam locomotion would go to the ranks of the ordinary, to the special PRR breed of tried-and-trusted locomotives with names like K4, L1, M1, I1, H10, etc.

Entering the decade of the 1950s, the prime question on the PRR was no longer whether to continue any alliance with coal-burning locomotives, but for how long? The Railroad quickly concerned itself with utilizing the two-cylindered steam to supplement the diesels in key areas where traffic fluctuated. More important, the Railroad strived for the most efficient operation of the diesels, system-wide, ignoring the steam-era tradition of changing engines at division points. The search for an ideal electric freight locomotive that would take advantage of diesel locomotive technology and be mass produced at competitive cost to the diesel got hotter with the delivery of prototype locomotives from GE, Baldwin and Westinghouse. Many of the fabulous class M1a locomotives received new boilers into 1953; that is, until the first of 310 Electro Motive GP9s arrived from La Grange to get their knuckled grip on freight cars. Appropriately the last steam locomotive to be tested at the Locomotive Testing Plant was an M1a equipped with a device to aspirate cinders from the smokebox and return them to the firebox. Before class modifications could be made, however, the decision came out of Philadelphia not to spend further monies on steam, except for necessary running repairs to keep the needed ones in operation.

While we have concentrated on what I feel is the most important, and certainly the most fascinating, aspect of the Pennsylvania Railroad, that is, its motive power development, a roll call of the projects and changes that occurred on the Railroad in the post-war 1940s and 1950s could fill another book. There are some changes I should mention that reflected the tremendous technical and social revolution that occurred right after the war. For instance, the new Samuel Rea freight car repair shop, the nation's largest, at Hollidaysburg, Pa., and the tens of thousands of badly needed new and rebuilt freight cars it started sending into service. I think of the new Conway Yard, tripling the capacity of the old yard, one of several such projects to speed up freight along the PRR. Along with new and improved classification yards, the Railroad concentrated on modernizing many shops, committing three million dollars a year to this program. New passenger trains were put into service in an effort to lure travelers back off the new highways and away from the DC-6s. The speedy new *Congressionals* between New York and Washington received national acclaim in 1952, as well as the low center of gravity, lightweight *Keystone* and *Aerotrain* which followed in 1956. New passenger train support equipment (like mechanical car washers) were introduced, along with new stations and ticket offices. Altoona conversions included coffeeshop–tavern passenger cars, in an effort to provide more efficient, lower cost service. A giant new ore pier was built and several tunnels in Ohio were daylighted for higher and wider loads, along with welded rail and new bridges and viaducts.

The pioneering Truc Train piggyback service was launched in July 1954 leading to the creation of a national piggyback pool. There was also a drive to recapture LCL business. Fast new symbol trains like NS-8 joined the schedule hauling merchandise between Chicago and Louisville. Equally important, perhaps, were the new trains like CP-6 between Chicago, Youngstown and Pittsburgh which brought much needed empties eastward. And very unusual, though a sign of Pennsy's efforts to improve efficiency, was symbol DC-1, a healthy little hotshot that picked up outbound shipments from customers around Chicago and headed them west, directly to the line-haul railroads. The concept of DC-1 came out of one of the newly formed Saturday morning service meetings where Chicago traffic and transportation reps kicked around ways of improving PRR business. On a system-wide scale, new departments like Methods and Cost Control, and Community Relations were created. By 1955 the Pennsylvania had spent over a billion dollars on post-war improvements.

An enormous chapter in American railroading ended on November 27, 1957 with the arrival home in Altoona of I1sa #4271 on a coal train out of Cresson, Pa., off the Pittsburgh Division. That night the fire was dropped from the thirty-four-year-old Decapod at the East Altoona enginehouse, bringing steam locomotive operations on the Pennsylvania Railroad to an end. On November 28, 1957, the number 4271 was as much a part of history as engine #1, first used in 1857. In 1957 General Electric conducted a study of the PRR's motive power situation east of Enola. Among the study's findings was the fact that as many as forty-three diesels were substituting for failing electric locomotives on any given day. For the first time, there was serious talk in management about the possibility of de-energizing the electric freight operations and dieselizing. Interestingly enough, General Electric, EMD and Alco each studied Pennsy's electric operations in 1958 and into 1959, and they all agreed that continuation of the electrics would be better than dieselizing. Diesels, they reasoned, would not be able to meet the operational demands of the electrics, could not run as fast, and would cost more to operate. GE figured that it would take 377 diesel units to replace 150 electric freight locomotives.

By 1958 the tides of fortune were changing fast, and for the worse. President James Symes stood up in front of a Congressional sub-committee and said the Railroad was "deteriorating badly." The Company, he said, was "not a very attractive investment," and he emphasized that the post-war improvements were made possible only by deferring maintenance and divesting non-Railroad properties. On November 1, 1959, James M. Symes was named Chairman of the Board of Directors with Allen J. Greenough, former Vice President in charge of transportation and maintenance, succeeding Mr. Symes as President. The press release noted that Symes would "now be able to devote more time to national railroad affairs, which have become increasingly vital to the welfare and progress of the PRR and the entire industry." Although not regularly discussed on the public level, the one-time unimaginable, unthinkable scenario of Pennsy and New York Central discussing survival by merging the two properties had begun.

My role in writing this book has been that of preservationist, and my greatest pleasure has been in helping to recreate images of the Pennsylvania Railroad during the 1940s and 1950s. Returning to the era of the Pennsy after so many years is somewhat unsettling, and I've had to rely on written and oral accounts to give a true feeling of the time. But it has been memory—mine and that of others involved in the Railroad—which has played the greatest role in bringing back and preserving this very important time in our history. While there may be some important information missing, or even a wrong date, the attempt has been made to bring back the Pennsy—an American institution that mirrored this nation for well over one hundred years.

In 1871 a reporter from *Harper's Weekly* wrote about the drama of Pittsburgh: "The dense volumes of black smoke pouring from the hundreds of furnaces, the copious showers of soot, the constant rumbling of ponderous machinery, the clatter of wagons laden with iron." Anyone who had reason to pass through, live in, or visit Pittsburgh during the 1940s and 1950s knew that this description of the hub of the nation still held. The future seemed to emanate from the blast furnaces, the leaping flames from the Bessemer converters, the searing heat soaring out from white-hot steel ingots, the ever-present halo of gasses overhead, the constant roar from the din, the warning sirens for moving machinery. To the majority of us not familiar with the technical improvements within the steel-making industry, little had changed from the 1871 account. The clatter of wagons, of course, had been replaced by the locomotives and cars of the Pennsylvania Railroad. The PRR was everywhere, feverishly keeping pace with the process of the industrial output.

It is often said that in Pittsburgh the tempo of our industrial might was set by the steel mills. Here the iron and steel production went into high gear to build our factories, cities, and railroads. Here the role of the railroad in building this country was defined and put into action by the Pennsylvania Railroad. Pittsburgh and the PRR radically changed our lives, by bringing in raw materials to make finished products to ship throughout the nation. Within one generation, America became the mightiest and most self-sufficient industrial nation on earth.

At the outbreak of World War II the Pennsy's trackage accounted for a little over 6.5 percent of all the track in the country and yet it produced 11 percent of total revenue for the railroads. One out of every ten locomotives in the United States at that time belonged to the PRR, as did nearly 14 percent of the freight cars and over 15 percent of the passenger cars. Half of the population in the U.S. was served by the Pennsylvania Railroad. And I suspect that the Pennsy, more than any other American railroad, touched America's conscience, whether it was a Lionel GG1, an American Flyer K4, or a Norman Rockwell painting depicting a soda fountain with a Belpaire-boilered locomotive off in the background, some aspect of the Pennsy was etched on the American scene. After the war, one of the advertisements I distinctly remember was a Ditto Incorporated ad featuring an industrial artist's rendering of M1 locomotives running alongside a T1 (on freight) and an FT diesel (on passenger) past soaring buildings and even an oceanliner, with DC-4s flying overhead. All of this to dramatize big business, and its need for Ditto Business Systems. And of course, I should mention the big, wonderful PRR calendars which adorned walls everywhere, including my own. I would dare say the GG1 showed up over the years in more advertisements and movie clips than any other locomotive. And, of course, the rakish Loewy T1 surely came in for a close second in the media blitz (yes, I'd place Central's Dreyfus Hudsons, Santa Fe's Fs and Espee's Daylights in third, fourth, and fifth places). For people of all ages, the mighty Pennsylvania Railroad was *the* prestigious railroad to own in the game of Monopoly.

During the years documented in this book, we have stood trackside to witness two decades that, in retrospect, turned out to be the most decisive, most pivotal years for the Pennsylvania Railroad, and for America. In the immediate years after World War II, America turned in the greatest productive record of any nation in history. Coal, steel and iron production—the three indicators of our industrial strength—rose to the highest level in peacetime history. The 1929 benchmark rate of investment and capital formation was doubled in 1947, and the output of consumer goods rose to record levels as the nation re-geared for peacetime. And yes, the cost of doing business rose with (and in many cases exceeded) the income derived.

But at this time of great productivity, the Pennsy ceased calling itself "The Standard Railroad of the World." The mighty Railroad, as we knew it, was starting to die.

The end of steam was not the incredible duplexes, nor the steam turbine, but a two-cylindered tribute to the lasting designs of standardization, unscathed and proven over the years. In the mid-1950s, even the casual observer could see the difference in the style of the Railroad, be it single stripes (or no stripes) and keystone decals, to economy passenger trains, trailers riding flat cars, and quiet and layoffs at Altoona. The hundred plus years accumulation of cinders along Horseshoe were the remains in the ascent of time. Here and there, ghosts of past PRR generations presided over the property in the form of coaling docks, keystone-shaped whistle posts, 152 lb. rail, position light signals, custom diesels, etc., but we knew that the splendid days of nonconformity and indifference were gone. Toward the end, the sight of two I1s shoving hard on an N5, or an ageless GG1 rushing under the wires was glorified in the light of a setting sun.

As my work on this book comes to a close, I think back on the many conversations I had with men who were working for the Pennsylvania Railroad during the years covered here. Their words perhaps give the best indication of how the Railroad was different, insular, possessing a culture of its own. The Pennsylvania was, without a doubt, a no-nonsense, blue-collar railroad, as well as a vital force in industrial America. The Pennsy was grim, strong and dirty, as the pictures here prove. And the men who worked her were deeply committed to her. To the employees, the Pennsylvania Railroad was a way of life. Their recollections are so vivid, so wonderfully spicy and full of a sense of immediacy, that it is tempting to believe that nothing has changed, and that the Pennsy is still with us.

I talked with an engineer who remembered the six ponderous, low-drivered Norfolk & Western Y-3 mallets the Railroad got in 1943 to help with the war-laden traffic. "We got 'em off the Railroad," he recalled, "out of the way, and into the yards. We didn't have time for them!" On the Fort Wayne Division, an engineman used to love to "wake everyone up in Kosciusko County, tying the whistle down for thirteen grade crossings in Plymouth, Indiana." Also on the Fort Wayne an inspector who was assigned to the AAR test train for high speed passenger car evaluation talked about the K4s and E6s. "The Railroad always wanted an E6 for speeds over 100 miles per hour. We would get out of Fort Wayne," he reminisced, "just ahead of the Blue Ribbons, and run like hell. One K4 couldn't do what an E6 could do on the four-car train. The K4's main pins wouldn't take it, and it was hard to keep up steam. At 100, your fire just danced in the E6, two guys taking turns with the scoop."

A tower operator reminisced about the new Q2 locomotives on the property and how he would time his drive home after duty to watch one whenever possible. "Oh, they'd run, I'll say that! I used to see the head brakeman up in the doghouse hanging out, looking back over the train on the curve. Oh, they did run—get on a country road and pace 'em. Hardly looked like the engine was running, until you looked at those small rods—and your speedometer."

Back East, an engineer commented on the GG1, specifically the notch limiter, and referred to the routine performance of the Gs out of Penn Station, New York. "Coming up grade with eighteen heavy weight pullmans on a short time overload, amounting to 8000 horsepower—that's pretty fantastic!" Another guy from the Test Department, musing over the times when increasing war traffic made it difficult to "get the Railroad for testing," remarked: "The traffic tore up the railroad—and many locomotives. Back east, the Gs . . . ah, the Gs—they just kept at it. Thank God for the GG1!"

In April of 1954 I made a spring weekend trip to De Pauw University in Greencastle, Ind., to visit my sister and look over the school. After a hectic Saturday, seeing the dean of admissions, campus, classrooms, fraternity houses, and attending a dinner and dance, I slept in the Lamda Chi house. Sometime during the night I was awakened by the racket of a steam locomotive on the nearby Pennsylvania Railroad. An eastbound freight had made a stop at the water plug just beyond the East Washington Street crossing and was having difficulty getting started up the grade and out of town. I lay in the dark and listened to the struggle. After several slips, the train was finally underway, the whole engine tightening in the endeavor, as engineer and firemen were crowding the boundaries of her capacity. I listened for several minutes until the engine finally settled in her stride, and the following cars finally rolled out of hearing distance. I heard her mellow whistle blow for a crossing somewhere east of town, and a sense of contentment came over me; a battle had been won, and I felt assured that all was well.

Summary of dynamometer road tests conducted on the Norfolk & Western with Pennsylvania T1 locomotive no. 5511 and Norfolk & Western class J locomotive no. 604.

In connection with a test by the PRR of an N&W class Y-6 locomotive; arrangements were made to test a class T1 in August 1948 to develop the comparative performance and economies of the T1 and class J locomotives. Tests were set up in heavy grade territory on the Radford Division between Roanoke, Elliston and Christiansburg, Va. and in low grade, high speed territory, on the Norfolk Division between Poe and Suffolk, Va. Between Roanoke and Christiansburg a train of 15 passenger cars and the dynamometer car, for a total of approximately 1065 tons, was used behind the class J. For some of the runs, loaded coal hoppers were added between Elliston and Christiansburg to bring the train weight up to 1758 tons. For the test runs with the T1 locomotive, 13 passenger cars and the dynamometer car were used, for a total of approximately 1003 tons. For some of the runs, loaded coal hoppers were added at Elliston to increase the trains' weight to 1220 tons (a train weighing 1440 tons was tried with the T1, but a stall occurred soon after the entire train was on the 1.32% grade out of Elliston). For the medium to high speed runs, both locomotives handled twenty passenger cars plus the dynamometer car, weighing approximately 1506 tons. Tests were run at three different sustained speeds of 65, 75, and 85 mph. Standard procedure on the tests was to accelerate the train to the desired speed as fast as possible and then maintain the speed. One speed restriction of 45 mph was posted at Waverly, allowing for a second fast, monitored acceleration back up to the correct top speed. At all but the top speed range, the T1 showed poorer fuel consumption and quantity of steam required per unit of work than the class J. At 75 mph, the T1 started to use less steam per drawbar horsepower than the J, but still was not as efficient in the production of steam. Maximum recorded drawbar horsepower for the J was a little over 5100 at 40 mph, while the T1's was approximately 4600 at 55 mph. Unlike the J's horsepower rating that dropped off rapidly at higher speeds, the T1's horsepower remained fairly consistent up to 90 mph. J. M. Moseley, Research and Test Engineer for the N&W summed up the tests of the two locomotives in his September 21, 1948 internal memorandum stating, "The class T1 showed up unfavorably by comparison with the class J at other than high speeds. In normal operation on the N&W and, we believe, on most roads, there is not enough uninterrupted running at high speeds to offset the large disadvantage shown for the high wheel, short stroke T1 locomotive when handling trains on medium to heavy grades, when accelerating from starts and slow down, and when runing in rolling or light grade territory at medium speeds." For all of the test runs with both locomotives, assigned crews of engineers and firemen were used to obtain consistent operation. Coal for each comparative test between each locomotive was used from the same mine.

Summary of dynamometer road tests conducted on the Norfolk & Western with Pennsylvania Q2 locomotive no. 6180 and Norfolk & Western class A locomotive no. 1210.

On August 2, 1948, PRR class Q2 locomotive no. 6180 was delivered to the Norfolk & Western at Columbus, Ohio for evaluation tests over the low grade Kenova District. Official performance data rated the Q2's starting tractive effort without booster at 100,800 pounds as compared with 114,000 pounds for the class A. With booster, the Q2 was rated at 115,800 pounds starting tractive effort—11.58% less TE than the A without booster; 1.58% more TE with booster. Three westbound trips with 11,500 ton coal trains and three eastbound trips with 175 empty hoppers were conducted. Prior to the tests, the Q2 was shopped at Portsmouth Roundhouse and the dynamometer car and engine were instrumented. On all trips, PRR Road Foreman Guy Harding fired with either N&W Assistant Road Foremen Morgan or Arrington running, to obtain uniform results. On all trips the Q2 required more steam per unit of work than class A test locomotive no. 1210, resulting in the use of more fuel per unit of work. The Q2 handled the eastbound empties between Portsmouth and Williamson at an average speed of 28.10 mph, including the coal stop at Prichard. Data obtained from identical tests with class A locomotive no. 1210 showed the N&W engine handling the same train at an average speed of 31.7 mph, using 31.40% less dry coal per drawbar horsepower. Thermal efficiency was much lower on the Q2 than the A. The biggest complaint was the tendency of the Q2's front engine to slip with the consequential loss of otherwise available steam chest pressure. The Q2's slip control device would not function properly (this came as no surprise) on most of the runs. In short, the more the work required, the more the A out-classed the Q2 in all categories. No. 6180 was returned to the PRR at Columbus following completion of the tests.

Condensed summary of tests conducted on the Chesapeake and Ohio with Pennsylvania T1 class locomotive equipped with poppet valves.

The C&O was interested in the PRR's class T1 locomotive, which incorporated a large boiler, high drive wheels, poppet valves, and heavy weight as a design that might be successful in handling passenger trains in mountain regions as well as in non-mountainous terrains. Pennsylvania's T1 locomotive no. 5511 was received by the C&O at Cincinnati on September 4, 1946. The dynamometer car was coupled directly behind the test locomotive and instrumented for drawbar pull, speed, and record of mile post location. The amount of coal and water used on each trip was estimated by one of the traveling engineers from the Pennsylvania Railroad.

The C&O was aware that that T1 was designed to handle a maximum trailing load of 880 tons at 100 mph on level, tangent track, and given the characteristics of their railroad knew it was not possible to test the Pennsylvania locomotive at its designed speed. No. 5511 was tested from Huntington, W.Va. to Clifton Forge, Va., Clifton Forge to Toledo, Ohio, and Toledo to Hinton, W.Va. On September 8, the PRR recalled the 5511 and sent the 5539 as a replacement. Tests were resumed on September 11 with the balance of the testing conducted between Huntington and Charlottesville, and Charlottesville and Cincinnati. The 5539 spent most of its time on the C&O handling both the *George Washington* and the *FFV*. Engineers complained of extremely slow starts without booster, and slow acceleration with the 80-inch drivers, in spite of the fact the C&O used 78-inch drivered 4-6-4s.

On September 12, the 5539 was assigned to no. 46, *The Sportsman* eastbound from Clifton Forge to Charlottesville over the Mountain Sub Division. The train's consist was thirteen cars and 1098 tons. At Waynesboro, Va. No. 46 made its station stop on time, but getting underway on the 1.31% grade out of the station was another matter. After much slipping, burning rail, and, as train crew members reported, "much coffee slopping in the diner," a pusher was called to get the train started. A quick turn around was made at Charlottesville to get the T1 on train no. 1, the *George Washington*, over the Mountain Sub Division and Allegheny Sub Division to Hinton. No. 5539 made its station stop at Craigsville, Va. and once again got hung up, this time with eleven cars and 946 tons of train on the 1.44% grade. After ten minutes of wild slipping and back sanding, the traveling engineer got the *George* underway. Once again, scuttlebutt got around the railroad about how rough the ordeal was for the passengers and the men working the diner. On the ensuing grade out of Craigsville, the dynamometer car recorded a top horsepower output of 5012 at 6½ mph, attaining a very respectable 57,026 pounds of tractive effort. The big duplex cooled her wheels the next day and was returned to the PRR on September 14. The C&O T-1 on the Pennsy turned out to be the bargain!

Trackside   1940s – 1950s

39

It wouldn't be right to open up an east-to-west volume on the Pennsylvania Railroad without a brief look at the New Haven Railroad over whose rails PRR trains operate and vice versa. At upper left, brand new EP-5 ignitron rectifier locomotive #373 sands the rails, getting the westbound *Senator* underway toward New York, out of Stamford, Ct. The beautiful train will cross over from track 3 onto track 1 where it will run down to New Rochelle and then cut over on the Hell Gate line that will take it into Pennsylvania Station. Below, EP-3 "flat bottom" #352 heads east through Bridgeport on a light move to New Haven. She is shown since it was sister locomotive #0354 that the PRR tested in 1933 that ultimately resulted in the design and construction of the GG1.

The Long Island Rail Road played a very important role in the history of the PRR, and is included in the form of Juniata-built G5s #24 heading a commuter train out of Oyster Bay, N.Y. The LIRR was incorporated on April 24, 1834, and figured a very important role in Pennsy's electrification plans into Manhattan. A majority of LIRR stock was acquired by the Pennsylvania in 1900 with electric service commencing by 1905. On November 27, 1910, when the magnificent Pennsylvania Station was opened in Manhattan, LIRR trains began service to Penn Station via tunnels under the East River. (Ball)

Sunnyside yard, located in Long Island City across the East River from Pennsylvania Station, is the largest of all passenger train yards. It is two miles long, serves over 100 trains each day, and is home for the commissary department, Pullman facilities and electric passenger locomotive servicing on the east end. Descriptions of this operation cannot do it justice! Plying Sunnyside's 44 miles of tracks and 296 switches are the unique B1 switchers built specifically for passenger yard switching. The #5691 pictured at Harrisburg (the "cat poles" give the location away) was one of fourteen B1s built by Altoona in 1934 and 1935, next to the first GG1s; a total of twenty-eight B1s were built. At upper left, we see the servicing of DD1 electric locomotives once used between Penn Station and Manhattan Transfer in New Jersey, before the 11,000-volt mainline electrification in the 1930s. Thirty-three double unit, DD-class locomotives were built at the Juniata Shops between 1909 and 1911 for the 650-volt d.c. third rail operation; these units now survive to handle work trains in the river tunnels, using the third rail under de-energized catenary. At lower left, and in the open area just west of Penn Station between Ninth and Tenth Avenues, Altoona-built L6 motor #5939 switches Penn Station. She was built in 1932, one year after New Haven's GE-built EP-3, seen laying over in Yard A to handle a Boston train to New Haven. (Van Dusen, Ball collection; Tatnall; Ball)

In early 1901, the Pennsylvania Railroad started studying the possibility of tunneling under the Hudson River and right into Manhattan. On July 1, 1904, actual work began, including excavation on an eight-acre site for the magnificent Pennsylvania Station. The station building was Roman Doric with a great vaulted hall patterned after the Roman baths of Caracalla for the main waiting room. Under the huge station lies 28 acres of track and platforms. We can see here some glimpses of busy Penn Station, including the Seventh Avenue main entrance with its generous two-block long colonnade of Doric columns, and other accoutrements, the great concourse inspired by the Basilica of Constantine, a ticket window, and, of course, an inbound and an outbound GG1 hauled train.

This midtown monument to the great Pennsylvania Railroad was designed by the architectural firm of McKim, Mead & White. The station, tunnels, and electrification work was of such unprecedented magnitude that the *New York Times* obliged itself to keep the public posted on the progress of the station project for several years. (#4889-Sweetland; waiting room-Tatnall; all others-Ball)

The Electric Highway of the PRR! We're riding in 477,000 pounds of GG1, spread out over twenty wheels, gliding effortlessly down the 152-pound jointed rail of the New York Region main. Behind us, and stretched out on the curve, coming out of Bergen Hill Tunnel are eighteen tuscan cars. Under us is a continuous fill across the meadows made from most of the 3.5 million tons of subsoil that was excavated for the building of Penn Station. (What wasn't needed for the two track fill was put to good use in the then new Greenville yard, back in 1907.) Speed is up to 80 now, mere child's play for our GG1. We're riding in one of 139 streamlined GG1 electrics that could very well claim the title of finest and most famous locomotives in the world. Ahead, signal bridge 38.37 and a *clear* indication. The number 1 pantograph rides the 11,000-volt contact wire suspended from a web over us – a lifeline web of power extending over 2,228 track miles and 664 route miles. In a couple of miles we'll have a speed restriction over the Hackensack River draw since it is supported on pilings that do not reach bedrock until at least 100 feet down. Our station stop at Newark is four miles beyond.

Lehigh Valley trains get in and out of New York via the PRR from the Waverly Avenue interchange in Newark, where power is exchanged between the two railroads. At upper right, we're now in the cab of GG1 #4899, arriving with train No. 9, the *Black Diamond*, at *NK* tower and the interchange with the Valley. Lehigh Valley's PA diesels #604 and #608 in the siding will take over for the run to Buffalo. At lower right, we have left our G and depart for Buffalo in the cab of PA #608. The raucous sound of our turbocharged 16-cylinder 244 engines makes the silent power of the GG1 seem unreal. (Ball)

47

At the lower left, we're at milepost 14.12, standing on the wooden platform in Elizabeth, N.J. An approaching light, then a blast on the single note horn of GG1 No. 4877 tells us to step back from No. 4 track; she's bearing down on us fast with *The Embassy* for Washington. A combination of tuscan parlor cars, buffet lounge, dining car and coaches roars past and disappears off the "S" curve. Above, and on

another nice day, tail car, "Mountain View," passes over West Jersey Street and wraps the Chicago bound *Broadway Limited* around the "S" curve at Elizabeth, the GG1 on the point approaching *Elmora* tower's interlocking. By the looks of things in "Views" buffet-lounge-obs, the double bedroom and both master rooms are sold out tonight.

At upper left, and because I like Fairbanks-Morse Train Masters, here's a Jersey Central TM heading a Bay Head bound train down the PRR with the apparent urgency of Pennsy's operating schedules. In a book dealing with the PRR in the 1940s and 1950s, this may be taking a little literary license, but look at the flying 2412 again – can you *really* complain? (Ball, Kring, Landau)

The Pennsylvania Railroad, like most large railroads, is comprised of hundreds of separate corporations, controlled through ownership of stock or under long term leases. Most of these corporations exist in name only, and are unknown as separate entities, unless, of course, you work for the Company's finance department. A good example is the 6.54 mile Perth Amboy & Woodbridge Railroad from the main at Rahway to Perth Amboy and the Jersey Central connection, where both Pennsy and CNJ combine to form the 39.45 mile New York & Long Branch Railroad to Bay Head. At South Amboy, where electric operations end and PRR steam and diesel operations begin, is one of the finest action-packed rail theaters in the land. By way of example, we show, at lower left, MP54s heading toward New York City while GG1 #4936 waits to cross over to the "MU running track" after bringing in the train (at right) from New York. At upper right, Jersey Central's last Train Master, out of a lucky fleet of thirteen, roars through town non-stop, with a train for Bay Head, while a set of PAs wait for the GG1 from New York to cut off their train. The tracks off to the left belong to the Raritan River Rail Road interchange with the Jersey Central. There is also a connection with the PRR off the Camden & Amboy at RRRR Jct., about a mile away. In a few minutes, the AP-20 Alcos 5752 and 5753 pass us wide open in 8th notch throttle, the turbo not caught up with the engine speed yet, blasting partially burned fuel out of both stacks from roaring V16s. The closing picture, at upper left, shows a K4s heading down to the trailer track to wait for its train from New York. (Left page-Cohen; right page-Raymus)

The urban and pastoral character of the New York & Long Branch is reflected on this spread. At upper left, tuscan red E7 (known as an EP-20 on the Railroad) #5881 hurries a midday train, ducking under the new Garden State Parkway bridge at Hazlet in the process. The 5881 was built in 1948 and was one of four A units (out of 46) that never received MU connections. The other "untouched noses" belong to 5871, 5872, and 5874. Lift rings were installed along with different louvers and additional air intakes. At lower left, and quite frankly more my cup of tea, K4s #3747 has a good wheel on train No.748 up the grade north of Matawan in the late afternoon sun. In about ten minutes she'll arrive at South Amboy where a GG1 will take over for the run into New York. At upper right one of Jersey Central's distinct Baldwin DR-6-4-2000 double-ender diesels (in this case #2000) built in 1948 heads a Jersey City train up the middle track through South Amboy. Those passengers headed for New York will change to the Liberty Street Ferry (at Jersey City) for the 12-minute ferry trip across the Hudson River. At right, the sun glints off the top of the cast iron base of the manual crossing gate guarding the north side of John Street in South Amboy. Such relics as hand-me-down power, hand-operated crossing gates, wooden stations and towers, make the New York & Long Branch quite unique in its small-big-little railroad character. (CNJ-Brown, Ball collection; all others, Ball)

Hand me down power: basic, classic, angular, rakish, tough! There are many appropriate words for the endearing and enduring K4s locomotive, but the fact is, the K4s is a no-frills, well-balanced Betsy, built initially in 1914 as the standard express passenger locomotive to haul passenger trains at high speed over the entire PRR system. They now wear a coat of grime, these middle-aged machines, heroes of another time, and the stain of neglect shows in their rusting exterior. Watching K4s #5732 approach and pass, it strikes me how astonishing it is to see it adapt to the role of get up and go, then stop and go commuter service! Adapt it has, and once again, the assignment handed this great engine seems to be a good one. Incredible! (Obviously all of these things must have been expected of the K4s, for a total of 425 were built over a period of eighteen years.) P70s are on the drawbar, departing South Amboy this lovely winter evening.

At the lower left, and in the relative quiet of midday, a Bay Head train amply powered with two AP-20s appears along the shoreline of the Raritan River two minutes out of South Amboy. At right, The Baldwin BP-20 A-unit #5782, my favorite diesel passenger hauler on the Pennsy, heads a short Sunday afternoon train across the Navesink River into Red Bank. The icy wind is from the west and soon the river will be churning with white caps. It will become a battle of endurance against the biting wind, waiting to photograph the next train! (Cohen, Ball, Tatnall)

To the PRR "The Standard Railroad of the World," is not merely a slogan but the truth. The standard bearer for this notabene during the years of its greatness was the Railroad's K4s locomotive, pictured on this spread. As Webster puts it, in his definition of standard, "a conspicuous object (as a banner) formally used at the top of a pole to mark a rallying point . . . to serve as an emblem. . . . Something established by authority, custom, or general consent as a model or example."

Any way you slice it, the definitions work, for the 1914 K4s was born of an age of evolution to larger locomotives, outshopped by the hundreds during the time 4-6-4s and even 4-8-4s were rolling out of Baldwin and American. For thirty years, since the first production K4s engines arrived on the property in 1917, they marked the passage of Pennsy's tuscan trains. One of the keystones of the PRR's conservative motive power policy was to always obtain the maximum horsepower per axle consistent with tractive effort requirements, while at the same time adhering to mechanical designs that permitted interchangeability of parts with other locomotive classes. Add to this the need of a design that can be mass produced at reasonable cost, and the criterion of design becomes a little more exacting. The K4s was the natural evolution from the fabulous E6s class 4-4-2 during a time when passenger equipment was getting heavier and trains longer.

So now, in 1956, we pay tribute to this great engine. She has received modifications, of course, but she is still the same masterful piece of engineering introduced in 1914. In a way, (though these particular angles do not really show it), she looks like a great cat – a Jaguar, perhaps. The angular K4 is muscular at rest, seemingly tense, and quick to bound. When she's at stride, she looks lean and lithe. She is amazingly adaptable.

At lower left, it is 5:07 PM and K4s #646 gets the signal to depart Harborside Terminal in Jersey City for Newark with the *Broker*. After the 5:20 PM Newark stop, she will highball "under the wires" to Rahway and *Union* Interlocking where she will head down the Perth Amboy and Woodbridge Branch to Perth Amboy and the run down the Long Branch to Bay Head Junction. When Pennsylvania Station opened in Manhattan, the Harborside facility in Jersey City lost its mainline status, being relegated to a commuter station for Jersey City riders. In the middle, a close up look at K4s #5367 starting to back down to her train at South Amboy. Common practice is to watch the headlight of the GG1 that is being cut off. Once the motor is off No. 1 track and over on the middle, it is time to quickly back down to the waiting train.

At the lower right, the open fire doors on K4s #3856 at the South Amboy engine terminal showing a portion of the feedwater delivery system which is mounted on the backhead of the boiler. Common practice on other railroads is to mount it on the side. (Ball)

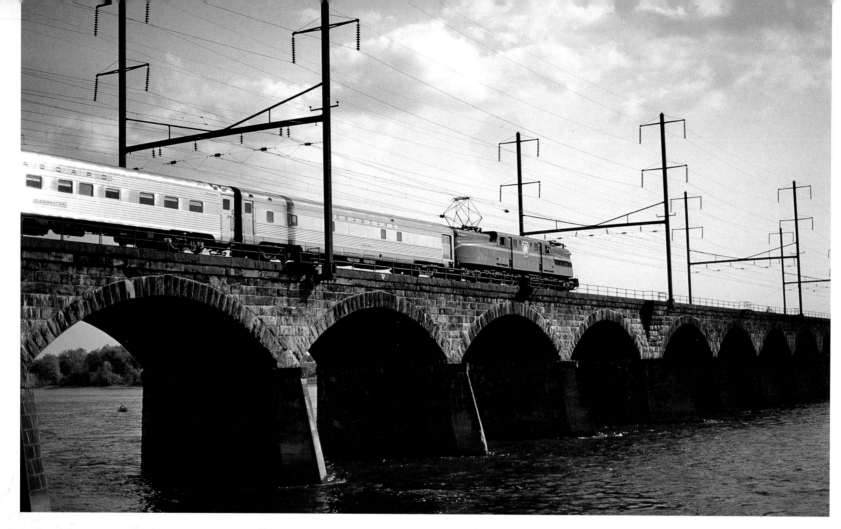

In 1887, the Pennsylvania Railroad undertook a massive program to rebuild most of its major bridges, under the direction of the Company's chief engineer, William H. Brown. The program called for stone masonry bridges because, ironically, it was felt that the massive stonework bridges were much stronger and more durable than steel, and certainly safer than iron or wood. Mother Nature perhaps proved a point after the PRR's first iron bridge at Johnstown, Pa., was replaced by stone spans which withstood the great Johnstown flood of May 31, 1889.

A bridge that deserves a degree of immortality is the graceful eighteen-span stone bridge between Trenton, N.J., and Morrisville, Pa., across the Delaware River on the New York to Philadelphia main line. In the lovely golden afternoon light of early spring, a tuscan GG1 glides across the graceful stone bridge out of Trenton, N.J., and into Pennsylvania with Seaboard's Florida bound *Silver Meteor*.

The clouds dissipate in the cool air as the sun loses its warmth and a *Clocker* heads for Philadelphia. Interesting that the Seaboard was the first railroad to receive streamlined equipment for Florida service back in February 1939, as well as some of the last post-World War II sleepers from both Budd and Pullman. This day we have equipment from both orders on the *Meteor*. (Tatnall)

Not many Princetonians are really familiar with the Standard Railroad of the World, but mention the "Dinky," or the "PJ&B" (Princeton Junction & Back) and they speak fondly of "their railroad"! In fact, some college students have stolen the MP54 on one or more occasions for joy rides. We begin this spread, at upper left, with the standard train on the "PJ&B," laying over in Princeton for the next departure to the main line two miles away at Princeton Junction. Not just an ordinary MP54, at that, but an MP54eg one of fifty rebuilt from steam coaches in 1950 for electric service. The cast steel trucks in lieu of the normal fabricated trucks give the cars' ancestry away.

Above right, and a quick 37.5 miles down the main line, a *Clocker* from New York makes its station stop at North Philadelphia Station enroute to Thirtieth Street Station. When the Pennsylvania Station opened in New York on November 27, 1910, the hourly service between New York and Philadelphia commenced, and these express trains between the two cities evolved into *Clockers* during the ensuing years.

At right, GG1 #4907 waits with the *Afternoon Congressional* for the conductor's highball. While immediately below, GG1 #4872, one of three silver-painted GG1s, heads the *West Coast Champion* from New York, en route to Washington, Richmond, Jacksonville, and St. Pete. The other silver GG1s are the 4880 and the 4866.

Last, the parlor-bar-observation car, "George Washington," brings up the markers of the *Afternoon Congressional* from Washington to New York. The "Congo" will overtake the slower *Montrealer*, five minutes ahead, also headed for New York and, of course, Canada. (MP54eg-Ball; all others-Tatnall)

North Philadelphia Station is too much of a hot spot on the Railroad to cover on just one spread. All north–south trains pass through North Philadelphia along with westbound trains that leave the New York–Washington corridor at *Zoo* tower interlocking just north of Thirtieth Street Station. In addition, South Jersey trains pass through, joining the main line at Frankford Junction, 3.2 miles to the north. Also, the busy Chestnut Hill Branch comes out of the suburban station in Philadelphia, and branches off at the North Philadelphia Station, contributing to the action. On this spread, we are witnessing change along the PRR as the tubular, low center-of-gravity *Keystone* arrives from New York, at left, with two head end cars and a G equipped with a test Faively pantograph under evaluation for possible future use; #4899 is the only motor so equipped. At upper right, K4s #5351 makes its early evening station stop, returning from the Garden State Race Track with a race train for Philadelphia. The mail in the foreground awaits the following *Broadway Limited* and its RPO car.

At lower right, two Alco AFP-20 dual-service, regeared PA diesels head PT-85 through North Philadelphia on No. 3 track, from Pavonia Yard, Camden, to Greenwich yard in South Philadelphia. You can expect any kind of power on this train.

At lower left, and earlier in the day, two recently delivered Alco AS-18m diesels rumble by with a lengthy BL-5 from Phillipsburg, N.J., en route to Edge Moor yard with a Bel Del train. (K4s – Tatnall; all others-Ball)

On this page, Broad Street Station in Center city Philadelphia and the typical MP54 trains that frequent the station. The Broad Street Station project was begun in 1881 with different architects working on the station over a period of years. Its 300-foot wide single-span train shed (which replaced the original twin spans) was the largest such single span in the world, when completed in 1893. Architects Joseph Wilson and Arthur Truscott were the first to work on the station, followed by Allan Evans and Frank Furness in 1893. Two fun things about Broad Street Station are the totally individual, competing towers that were built by Truscott, and later, Furness—both completely out of character with each other, and with the huge City Hall tower across the street.

When the station project began, the PRR was pondering the plausibility of electrification and in 1894 made some surveys to deter-mine costs of electrifying some of its local passenger service routes in nearby Camden. In 1895 the 7-mile Burlington to Mount Holly Branch was electrified with 500-volt d.c., with a resultant reduction of five minutes off the steam schedule and a nickel off the fare! By around 1910, the passenger business was up with no signs of leveling off. Broad Street had stub end tracks and the ensuing bottleneck of trains getting out the way they came in to turn their locomotives became unbearable. PRR President James McCrea, called in electric railway consulting engineer George Gibbs, and serious thinking started on how to electrify the Railroad out of Broad Street. By this time, the brass in Philadelphia was very aware of the successful, clean, and fast electric service being operated by the New Haven, New York Central and their own Long Island Rail Road up in New York. This fact was quite evident when the PRR or-dered new coaches for steam-powered suburban service in 1910, choosing a 64-foot class P54 coach with reinforced underframes that could be converted to electric cars. The Pennsylvania was impressed with New Haven's a.c. electrifica-tion and with an eye towards possi-bly electrifying the Railroad as far as Pittsburgh, chose a.c. for its first installation, commencing in 1914 out to Paoli. Two P54 cars were converted with electrical gear and the Railroad asked for employees interested in "the new era of ser-vice" to familiarize themselves with these cars. Ninety-three more P54 cars were phased out of service and sent to Altoona for conversion to 11,000-volt a.c. service. On Satur-day, September 11, 1915, electric service began out of Paoli with a four-car set of MP54s to Broad Street Station. World War I inter-fered with electrifying the Chestnut Hill Branch, but in April 1918, the conversion was completed and Broad Street Station's bot-tleneck was eliminated.

At upper left, it is Sunday, April 13, 1947, and we have the "Off the Beaten Track Special" NRHS fan-trip ready to depart Broad Street Station behind the beautiful duo of E5s Atlantic #6538 and E6s Atlan-tic #6513. The train will be on five divisions plus numerous branches throughout the general Philadel-phia area, and will cost a nominal $3.75 per person. It will return at 6:42 PM (that's 6:42, not 6:45!). At lower left, two MP54s head into St. Martins and it's a Christmas card-like setting, having just crossed the Cresheim Creek Bridge. Above, and seemingly soaring through the air, a train of Philadelphia-bound commuters leaves St. Martins, rumbling high over the Cresheim Creek on the enormous bridge. (Cope; Tatnall; Tatnall)

If we're going to go on a fantrip in this book, we're going to go with class! And what more class can we come up with than two of Pennsy's beautiful class E Atlantics? We are on the April 13, 1947 fantrip (shown on the previous spread) about to depart from Broad Street Station. Today we have felt the roll of the speedsters on the main line towards Wilmington, picked up the Chester Creek Branch at Lamoken Street to head to WaWa and on to Westchester and Frazier, to take the Trenton Cut Off to Morrisville. Once again, we hit our stride on the main line to Monmouth Jct., where we went off on to the Jamesburg Branch, originally built as the (would you believe?) Freehold & Jamesburg Agricultural Railroad Co. (a corporate title, purchased by the PRR in 1874) to Jamesburg. Thence the Camden & Amboy to Bordentown, and on to Kinkora and Lewis on the Kinkora Branch; over the Union transportation to Pemberton, the Camden & Burlington County to Pensauken—and I hope you know the rest of the way! Clockwise from near right, the train is pictured en route on the Chester Creek Branch, heading over a steel deck bridge, and taking on water—all pictures taken near Lenni, Pa. At lower right, what many come for, the photo runby at Monmouth, and a chance to *really* see and hear the Atlantics up close.

Locomotive afficionados talk about locomotives constantly. Any locomotive afficionado at any railfan event can, and will, give you an instant précis of any locomotive; and rarely do more than say, two or three, ever agree. It is doubtful the faithful gathered on

this fantrip have any disagreement on their objects of affection, for we have two grand ladies, cloaked in shiny engine black, adorning freshly painted keystones and wearing deluxe gold lettering—engines that represented the epitome of one time general superintendent of motive power, Wallace W. Atterbury's policy of meeting ambitious ends with modest means. Specifically designing and building engines to do the same work as larger, heavier engines. Certainly, the E6s, the final version of Pennsy's 4-4-2 was more than just a successful locomotive. The E6s was the absolute embodiment of brilliant theory and design put into practice. She represents mechanical engineer Alfred W. Gibbs's genius, built into a compact, simple and

elegant machine. No stoker, no feedwater heater, no power reverse, just pure, proven Pennsy practice and practicality. As we watch and listen, we sense in their presence, the grace and purity of Altoona's turn-of-the-century designs. And yes, what it must have been like, seeing one or two of them heading the *Pennsylvania Special* between Jersey City and Chicago, in eighteen hours flat. Likewise, the grand and wonderful limiteds between New York and Washington, with 29-seat parlor-buffet lounge cars bearing names that reflected the professions of the clientele like the "Engineers Club," the "Lawyers Club," and the "Professional Club." Magnificent trains with soda fountain broiler cars and buf-

fet parlors such as the "Mask and Wig Club" and "Poor Richard Club," trailing open observation cars named for such Americans as "Alexander Hamilton" or "Thomas Jefferson." Yes, today is a special day for memories and new experiences as the exemplary Atlantics get their chance to define why the Pennsylvania Railroad once rostered 601 of the fast-stepping 4-4-2s.

For the record, E5s Atlantic #6538 was built in Juniata in August 1913 as #338 for the former New York, Philadelphia & Norfolk, and E6s Atlantic #6513 was built in April 1914 as NYP&A #13. Both engines were renumbered in August 1918 when the "Nippen-n" became part of the PRR. (Cope)

Philadelphia reflects the Pennsylvania Railroad's grand scale. The many rail lines around the city testify to the sheer size of the Railroad, but perhaps more exemplary is the colossal Pennsylvania Station at 30th Street (usually called Thirtieth Street Station) near downtown. The grand concourse, larger in cubic feet than Pennsylvania Station in New York, spans the platforms with its tremendous columns and lavish marble. The suburban trains are all operated from a separate level in the complex. The huge adjoining post office building also spans the tracks and platforms on the south side of the station. At the left, General Motors' lightweight *Aerotrain* departs Thirtieth Street for its daily roundtrip to Pittsburgh. EMD's 1200 horsepower class EP-12 cab unit #1000 heads the rough-riding lightweight out from under the station. The ten cars on this train are an adaptation of GM's bus body, riding on single-axle trucks. At the upper right, a B1 switcher makes up train No. 35, the *Pittsburgh Night Express*, shoving cars for the rear end onto the platform under the post office. The pre-war Pullman, "Colonial Trails," has a drawing room, three double bedrooms and a buffet lounge.

At lower right, *if* there is anything that possibly tarnishes the extraordinary service record of the GG1s, it would be their inability to digest certain kinds of fine wind-blown snow and ice particles, causing shorts in the traction motors. (Consider the fact that a GG1 ingests 50,000 cubic feet of air per minute!) This explains the appearance of the Atlantic Coast Line and Richmond, Fredericksburg & Potomac diesels under the wires at Thirtieth Street Station. They have handled their Florida trains from Jacksonville, Fla., and Richmond, Va., respectively, ignoring the change to electric power at Washington. (ACL and RF&P diesels-Grosselfinger; all others-Tatnall)

The complexity of the Pennsylvania Railroad's tremendous physical plant around Philadelphia is only partially depicted on this and some of the other spreads in this book. At upper left, a recently shopped and repainted GG1 makes its stately appearance on the High Line with an Army – Navy special from New York. That's Franklin Field on the left; below are the non-electrified leads, belonging to part of the 31st and Chestnut Streets yard along with the yard office. At lower left, two members of the indefatigable class of G motors head past tracks 20 through 37 of the Penn Coach yard with MD-6 from Pot yard to Waverly (Jersey City). The two-tone gray heavyweight pullman cars in the foreground will be part of a special train to Ft. Dix. The West Philadelphia High Line stretches over one and a half miles above the city streets at an elevation of approximately fifty feet. It was built in 1903 with 160 spans for freights from the Chesapeake Region, as well as the South Philadelphia yards and coal pier. At right, one of my favorite pictures in this book: a K4s steams up the 2,129-foot approach span leading to the Delair Bridge over the Delaware River and toward Camden with an extra for the Garden State Race Track. (Tatnall)

On the following page, and on one of those days that makes you glad you are alive, two GG1s, headed by the 4807, rumble off the Delair Bridge with MD-116 trailing through the Baltimore truss spans and over the swing bridge 50 feet above the Delaware River's mean high water. In a few feet, the train will leave the Philadelphia Terminal Division and swing onto the connecting Fish House Branch past *Jersey* tower that will lead to Pavonia yard in Camden. On the opposite page we find Baldwin-built H8s #2897 on an eastbound freight through Broadway Station in Camden, and not too far away, Juniata B6sb #4001 busy switching hoppers in the Camden freight yard. (Kozempel; Ball; Kring)

Here we have a brief glimpse at some of the not-so-standard railroading along the Pennsylvania, the Philadelphia & Camden Ferry Company, the Reading, and the Pennsylvania – Reading Seashore Lines. At upper left, Juniata-built E6s class Atlantic #6092 pops off at 205 pounds, ready to head out of Camden with a Wildwood train. The 80″ drivered machine was built in March 1914, and is eloquently, classically Pennsy in all respects. Her fabulous high-capacity boiler was used on 79 other sisters built by Juniata in 1914 (when most railroads were ordering 4-6-2s), as well as over 1,200 2-8-0s and 121 4-6-0s. The locomotive was originally #5142 on the PRR before joining the PRSL roster in April 1938. At middle left, the tugboat "Greensburg" is seen at Hoboken, N.J., where most big marine repairs are made to Pennsy's "navy." At the lower left, ferry boats of the Pennsylvania-owned Philadelphia & Camden Ferry Company that operate between Market Street, Philadelphia, at Milepost 0, and Federal Street, Camden, milepost 1.03, where PRSL rails take over. At the upper right, we watch PRR class B6sb switcher #6391 switching several of the Seashore's fleet of twelve RDCs. At lower right, Reading G1 class 4-6-2 #129 is on a train departing for Wildwood. The RDCs successfully cover the seashore service, as well as the Glassboro and Millville runs, each RDC averaging over 200 miles every day! (Cope; Sweetland; Cope; Tatnall; Cope)

A warm, hazy August day in Camden, N.J., finds both a PRR 4-6-2 and a Reading 4-6-2 heading out of the Camden engine house to take their trains to Ocean City and Atlantic City, respectively. We watch both of these locomotives with intense interest and no small respect, for they truly represent an American classic in railroad history – the Alpha and Omega, you might say, of the 4-6-2 type locomotives. K4s #1361, along with her 424 sisters, is undoubtedly the most famous Pennsylvania Railroad steam locomotive of the almost 25,000 that have graced Pennsy's rails. At this late date, she is to be considered a survivor, but she is inextricably tied up with the life and drama of the PRR, from oil headlamps and two world wars, to the age of streamlining, and diesels. If it is possible to combine function, balance, grace, and stamina into an energetic, tireless, and tough machine, then the K4s is it!

The last 4-6-2 Pacific type locomotives built in America are Reading's ten G-3 class engines constructed by the railroad in 1948, of which semi-streamlined #214, on the left, is an example. Though the Reading followed a 1916 design that incorporated 2,983 square feet of total heating surface and 25 by 28-inch cylinders, that's where any similarities between old and new stop. The G-3s carry a healthy 260 pounds of steam pressure, have larger superheaters, roller bearings, cross-counter-balanced main drivers with cast steel beds that have integral cast cylinders, and develop a robust 48,340 pounds of tractive effort. There is the inevitable axiom that the more modern the machine becomes, the more its purity dwindles. I believe this is the case with the G-3. There are exceptions, of course, and I would suggest the modernized K4s as a sterling example.

Both engines are now patriarchs of the jointly owned Pennsylvania-Reading Seashore Lines, although they are on a daily lease basis from the PRR and Reading. Two thirds of PRSL's stock is owned by the Pennsylvania with the remaining third interest belonging to the Reading. In typically confusing railroad fashion, all equipment owned by the PRSL that needs major repair work is divided up on a "two-for-one" basis that drives accountants and clerks nuts. For every three engines that require work off the property, say at Wilmington, Altoona, or Reading, two are handled by the Penn and one by the Reading! The same goes for heavy repairs on rolling stock. It was not unusual to see a Pennsy B6sb in Reading or an RDG coach in Wilmington!

This is 1955 on the PRSL and things are changing. The track pans at Ancora were removed last year due to high maintenance costs for a dwindling number of steam-ers. A K4s on a Wildwood express had to take water and would nor-mally pick up two to three thou-sand gallons on the fly. On the other hand, the G-3s, with their 12,500 and 13,500 gallon capacity tenders, can make the run without taking on water. At Atlantic City, however, the G-3 is too long for the 75-foot table and has to wye on the No. 8 track within the interlocking limits of *Atlantic* tower at the ter-minal. The crews feel the G-3s give the K4 a run for its money.

Camden is quite a railroad town, having enough freight and pas-senger business to support four yards. The Camden Yard, partially seen on these two pages, was origi-nally the Camden and Amboy's yard. The other three yards are Bulson Street in South Camden, Cooper's Point in North Camden, and of course, Pavonia Yard in East Camden. Up until the late 1930s, the Pennsy had huge shops in Pavonia for building and repairing cars. (Sweetland)

At left, local freight CB-20 tries to brighten things up a little, arriving in Pensauken, N.J., with an unusual tuscan red Baldwin in the lead. It is amazing and amusing that the VO-1000 was adorned in red to handle the elite assignment of switching Sunnyside Yard in New York! She still wears the "EY" New York Division assignment symbol on her pilot, though she is now residing in the Pavonia Yard in East Camden. CB-20 comes out of Pavonia each morning and works all of the local industries on the Pemberton Branch up to and including Fort Dix, the largest customer. The genealogy of the symbol "CB" goes back to when the railroad from Camden to Birmingham was built by the Camden and Burlington County Railroad with freights consequently carrying symbols for Camden and Burlington County. Out of Pemberton, CB-20 will be operating on the Union Transportation Company which leased the trackage from the PRR per an agreement drawn in 1888.

At Upper right, CB-20 is pictured on another day, getting underway across the Stiles Avenue crossing in Maple Shade, N.J., after setting out a hopper car at the Graham brick yard. PRR operating rules call for steam to be placed behind diesels whenever possible. K4s #5433 is the helper and the Baldwin is the road engine. For you fans of brick yards, the kilns are coal-fired and each bakes 90,000 bricks at 2000°F in one firing. At the lower right, freight extra #5918 is pictured heading up the Union Transportation's trackage through Lewis, N.J., en route to Fort Dix. The smoke at the head of the 44-car train is from H10s helper #8686. A U.S. Army diesel switcher resides in a one-stall enginehouse on the base to switch out the cars. At the lower left, the crossing guard protects River Road while Baldwin VO-1000 #5913 crosses the C&A to enter the connection to the Back Road on the first lap of its journey to Fort Dix with CB-20. *Cooper* tower controls the north end (railroad direction) of Pavonia yard. (Kozempel)

Under the able tutelage of chief mechanical engineer Axel S. Vogt, Altoona outshopped three class E1 Atlantics in 1899. These locomotives were designed with one objective clearly taking preference over all others, to *run fast* on level track in New Jersey where they could compete with the Reading's Atlantic City Railroad to Atlantic City. And run they did, easily handling 300-ton trains at 75 miles per hour and better. In 1910, mechanical engineer, Alfred W. Gibbs, finished perfecting his design, when the E6 Atlantic emerged from Altoona. After the PRR conducted three years of typically thorough testing, eighty E6 locomotives were constructed by Juniata for high speed main line service. At left, the E6s that made fame in 1927, racing from Washington to Manhattan Transfer with the films of "Lone Eagle" Charles Lindbergh's return from his heroic trans-Atlantic flight. Covering the 216 miles in 175 minutes, between Washington and New York while the pictures of Lindy's return were being developed on board, #460 got the films to the theaters in New York City before those that were sent by plane! She drowses on a Sunday afternoon at Pemberton, N.J., the "EA" and "CTE" assignment symbols on her pilot beam indicating that she is an Eastern Region Atlantic Division locomotive out of the Camden engine house.

To the right, some pastoral simplicities along the 14-mile Union Transportation Company in New Jersey with leased B6sb #5244. The scenes include the unloading of a tombstone at New Egypt, under the watchful supervision of Conductor Radon and Engineer Elmer Jones; the pose of "immortal engineer," departing New Egypt; and a pan, enroute, backing a box car of feed from the north end. The Brill gas car #4662 is pictured at Tom's River, N.J. — I assume, under the watchful eyes of the crew of the Navy K class reconnaissance blimp out of nearby Lakehurst Naval Air Station. (E6s-Ball; UTCO pan-Ball; gas car-Tatnall; all others-Kozempel)

Stand back and give the K4 some running room! As we watch the race of trains to the seashore, we realize that under the cacaphony of the K4s mounting their runs, we are witnessing a triumphant processional of engines that *still* can provide us with firsthand evidence, in the mid-1950s, of what Railroading on the PRR was like before the duplexes and diesels. Stand back we will, as this star-studded cast of monarchs come forth at terrific speed with all the gusto and vitality of youth, heading to and from "America's Playground." At upper left, K4s #5459 comes into the cross wind, moving 14 heavyweight cars of Shriners and horses toward Atlantic City near Winslow Jct. At lower left, a Philadelphia express roars over (and through) the track pans at Ancora, behind the 3806. On May 23, 1943, engine #3806 was at the head of the 15-car train No. 1080, when it left the rails at Delair, killing 14 and injuring 81 passengers. Excess speed on the sharp curve of the Minson connecting track was the cause. At upper right, #5022 cannot be stopped at ½₂₅₀ of a second, bearing down on the 130-pound rail through Winslow Jct., heading a long consist to Atlantic City. At the immediate right, engines 518 and 3655 raise both dust and spirits, moving the Shriners from the "Olika Temple" through Hammonton in an all C&O consist. The color of the line can only be matched in part by some of the train names that plied its rails: *The Nellie Bly, The Boardwalk Flyer, The Barnacle Bill, The Mermaid,* and a host of others. (Kozempel; Kozempel; Ball; Kozempel)

At upper left, shades of the Kansas Division abound as K4s #5459 heads a Shrine extra through Winslow Jct. en route to Atlantic City. The train with its off-line baggage car, horse cars, parlors, coaches, sleepers, diner and lounge car is on the Delaware River Railroad and Bridge Branch. Below, E units head off the Back Road at Pensauken via the Jordan-Pensauken Connecting track for Philadelphia with deadhead equipment from Fort Dix. At upper right, the southbound *Nellie Bly* from New York to Atlantic City bounds across the Delanco Bridge behind the standard Baldwin AS-16 road switcher. At lower right, Alcos in Brunswick and tuscan are about to cross over from No. 1 track to No. 2 track at *Jordan* to head up the connecting track to Pensauken and on up to Fort Dix with a troop train. The CT 220 from February 7, 1943 shows twenty-five extra passenger trains in and out of Fort Dix that day! Five of the trains were solid Erie Stillwell consists! (Kozempel; Kring; Kring; Kozempel)

By the late 1800s there was enough passenger business to the Jersey seashore resorts that the PRR controlled two lines between Camden and Atlantic City. One route, the wholly owned subsidiary, West Jersey and Seashore Railroad, went via Newfield; the other route, the former Camden and Atlantic, went via Winslow Jct. Competitor Reading also had a parallel route with its wholly owned Atlantic City Railroad. Toward the turn of the century, the Reading Railroad had the fastest engines and the most prestige. As was previously pointed out, it was Reading's high flying P-class Atlantics, and to a lesser extent, its D-class Americans that sent Pennsy's Chief Mechanical Engineer, Axel S. Vogt, to the drawing boards to come up with the road's first class Es in 1899 and 1900. More important, it was Pennsy's enviable position of having two high-density parallel lines that enabled the Railroad to go ahead and undertake a lengthy electrification project. The road they chose to electrify was the longer West Jersey route. When the line opened in 1906, between Camden and Atlantic City, it was the longest electrification of a steam railroad in North America. By 1906, 79 coaches, 6 mail-baggage, 2 baggage and 2 baggage-coaches were in operation on the 75-mile long 650-volt d.c. third rail system.

In a world much quieter than the seashore and certainly less urgent than the bustle of Camden and Philadelphia, the midday train from Camden to Hammonton chuffs out of Haddonfield station, between the quaint buildings and across Lincoln Avenue with its well-kept gates and white-painted cast iron cross bucks. Once the purebred E6s Atlantic and her two cars are by, the crossing watchman will raise the gates and go back to his old metal lawnchair next to his shanty. Haddonfield is an important station since all connections with and between Camden and Philadelphia trains are made here. Just ahead of the engine, on the engineer's side, is *Vernon* tower where trains headed for Philly switch onto the bridge line tracks.

The small 5-lever US & S machine in the tower controls the two switches and two signals and has one locking lever. At lower left, the ubiquitous PRSL class H9s teams up with Reading I-8sb camelback #1611 on train WY-34, "the sand hog," as employees call it, heading over Newton Creek between York-ship and Gloucester. WY-34s consist is sand from the sandpits at Mauricetown and Manumuskin that will be used for glass and building materials. The pair of 2-8-0s will take the heavy train to West Yard (Pavonia) and will head empties back to the pits tomorrow on WY-33.

Fortunes for the railroads changed over the next two decades with the building of the Delaware River highway bridge between Philadelphia and downtown Camden along with a massive highway building program in New Jersey that was unprecedented for any state its size. After four years of incredible bickering, politicking, and positioning, the combined Pennsylvania-Reading Seashore Lines was consummated, beginning operations on June 25, 1933. At lower right, a train of MUs heads westward near Pitman, N.J., en route from Millville to Camden.

At the upper right, G5s #5709 is seen heading a train out of Woodbury, N.J., in lieu of MUs. In 1948 the New Jersey PUC ordered all wooden passenger cars removed, and consequently, the steam-hauled train. The all-steel MUs that were built in later years are still in service, along with the wooden mail-baggage and baggage cars. In regard to the G5s class engine which was specifically designed by PRR mechanical engineer, William F. Kiesel, for commuter service, one engineman on the LIRR summed up what a G5s was good for: "They could really make a commuter train snort in a hurry!" The G5s were the heaviest and most powerful 4-6-0s ever built. (Cope)

Not-so-standard railroading appears on this spread, although everything is "routine" in this part of the country. Above, E6s #6086 surprises us, crossing over from the main to the Newfield Branch, near Pleasantville, N.J. covering for the out-of-service gas car on the Newfield Local out of Atlantic City. The electrified tracks in the foreground belong to the Shore Fast Line; the Camden-Atlantic City main is also visible. At left, an AC&S trolley heads out of Ocean City on the long trestle to Somers Point. John Stevenson & Co. built the wooden car in 1906. The PRR controlled line smacks (sort of) of Pennsy's control – from the yellow markers and tuscan sash, to work equipment numbered in the 497000 series! At upper right, Juniata's "children's book engine" A5s class 0-4-0 #1587 is seen at Atlantic City on her midday break. At lower right, a local freight comes against traffic at Newfield Jct. to head over to the main and into Atlantic City. ND bobber #203 brings up the markers. (Cope)

When talking about the Standard Railroad of the World, we usually use a litany of superlatives that frightens and awes. "The heaviest rail . . . the greatest number . . . the most electrified trackage . . . the biggest, the fastest, etc . . . " We do not remember daisies and weeds, 4-4-0s and car floats, such as are encountered on the Delmarva Division. Examples that come to mind are the Baldwin switchers at Little Ferry, Va., grabbing cars off the "Captain Edward Richardson" (just "The ER" to a Pennsy man) from Cape Charles, or the hard working L1 heading up from the Cape Charles car float interchange with reefers for Edge Moor yard in Wilmington.

Or a 1900 vintage 80″ drivered D16sb on a way freight – certainly a vital spark of life in a haunt of antiquity. She is pictured on the light rail of the Easton Branch at Easton, Md. And what about that K4 heading northward near Greenwood, Del. with a work train? So often we forget. (Car float-Sweetland; all others-Cope)

Look carefully; there's a lot of history here. At upper left, in a scene that smacks of eighteenth-century ancestry, Pennsy's motor train from Parkton crosses the cobblestones of Guilford Avenue, headed into Calvert Station, Baltimore. At upper right, and a little later, the Baldwin 1000 h.p. switcher is pulling the morning train out of Calvert's circa 1848 train shed. She will head to the yard near Pennsylvania Station and set out the train for the day. At lower right, an Alco AS-10 class RS-1 is seen leaving Ruxton, Md., en route to Baltimore on the former Northern Central – a railroad the Pennsy acquired in 1900 to gain access all the way to Harrisburg, Williamsport, and Sodus Point, N.Y. The substantial rock station is indicative of the Northern Central's one time opulence. (As a matter of interest, Abe Lincoln traveled through here in 1863, enroute to deliver his Gettysburg address.) Meanwhile, back in Baltimore, we take a look at street tractor #446, at lower left, an Altoona-built rubber-tired gas-electric gismo with railroad couplers, grab irons, footboards, and airbrakes for switching the tight trackage around the eighteenth-century laid-out streets in the Fells Point waterfront area. The tractor is steered with a huge vertically mounted wheel, not unlike the helm of a great clipper ship. Incidentally, the Maryland state flag, which antedates Old Glory, has the founding Calvert family coat of arms and is the only heraldic state flag in the United States. (Tatnall)

It has been said, that Raymond Loewy's first design project for the Pennsylvania Railroad was to modernize the trash cans in New York's Pennsylvania Station. I have to assume this first assignment was a success, for Loewy's second project was to consult with Fred W. Hankins, Chief of Motive Power in 1934 on doing an aerodynamically streamlined body shell for the new GG1 electric locomotives that were coming soon for the rapidly increasing New York – Washington passenger business. The rest is history and it is now time to savor the fruits of Loewy's labors.

At top left, the ageless queen of electrics in its traditional high speed pose rolls a brand new *Afternoon Congressional* toward Washington, racing the setting sun near Aberdeen, Maryland. In a mile she'll roar through town and across a main street still protected by manual crossing gates. At left center, motors 4910 and 4913 cross the graceful viaduct at West Manayunk, Pa., with a train of Boy Scouts bound for the Jamboree at Valley Forge. At lower left, heavy oil smoke comes out of the steam heat boiler stack as the 4912 is readied at Ivy City to take a train to New York. To the right, the 4912 is seen on another day at bumper post's end at Washington Union Station with the *Morning Congressional*. Motor #4910 was built by Altoona in 1941; the GG1s, 4911 through 4913, represented on this spread, followed in 1942. (Cohen; Kring; Van Dusen, Ball collection; Ball)

The Main Line, to both railroader and Philadelphian alike, refers to the upper-class suburbs west of Philadelphia where a lifestyle of wealth and tradition flourishes. The trustees of Philadelphia, like those of Boston, invested the old family fortunes with extreme conservatism, namely in real estate along the Main Line. (It is said a sound mortgage was venerated in Philadelphia practically on the same level as the Episcopal Church.) Along the Main Line, the Tracy Lords of the *Philadelphia Story* perpetuate a life of debutantes, thoroughbreds, dinner dances, vestry manners, the Shipley School, and Bryn Mawr.

Along the Main Line of the *Railroad*, the Pennsylvania perpetuates itself in the form of tuscan and tonnage, busily using the four track Main around the clock. By way of example, three P5A motors grind westbound upgrade through Merion, Pa., with a heavy ore train, while five miles further west, we catch the rear end of the same train at Rosemont, being pushed by two Baldwin BS-24s that got into the act at *Arsenal* tower in South Philadelphia. The tri-mount trucks, in lieu of the Commonwealth GSC trucks, give away the fact that these engines were built during Baldwin's final years. The Pennsy owned 23 out of the 24 BS-24s (Baldwin called them RT624s) with the Minneapolis, Northfield & Southern getting the 24th unit.

At the lower right, the GG1's ugly sister, and the one and only DD2 motor, #5800, is seen leaving Greenwich yard, Philadelphia, with a cabin. When the PRR seriously thought they were going to electrify the Middle and Pittsburgh divisions, the DD2 was constructed by Altoona in 1938. She was supposed to be a dual-service machine, having four P5a traction motors and 72" drivers, producing a formidable 5000 horsepower. Alas, time and events were not on her side. (Tatnall)

We have talked about the Main Line and the Railroad's early views of electrification and its expense relative to steam operations. Perhaps the official handwriting on the wall for steam, and maybe even the electrics, came in the Company's 1948 annual report, which stated: "The ton-miles of service per locomotive-hour produced by these engines (the new diesels) so far surpasses the performance of any previous type of motive power."

At upper left, and most likely *not* the "new diesels" the Railroad was touting in 1948, sixteen Westinghouse 370F traction motors grind away, pouring close to 150,000 pounds of continuous tractive effort onto the rail through 32 wheels in the form of a monstrous Baldwin BH-50 centipede diesel. The coupled set is shoving a westbound ore train out of Pier 122 in South Philadelphia, bound for their biggest customer, U.S. Steel at Saxonburg, Pa., on the B&LE. At lower left, an Alco A-B-A lashup of AF-16s gets into the act roaring westward along the Main Line through Rosemont with a train out of Camden about to overtake a local. Next stop for the Paoli local is Villanova, 1.1 miles away – enough distance to catch up with the freight for a few seconds. At upper right, a single P5a handles empty hoppers west from the coal pier in South Philadelphia. The train is passing through Haverford. At the lower right, General Electric's entry into the new freight locomotive design competition that the Railroad solicited bids for in 1949 is the E2b. This straight a.c. double-unit locomotive has 48" drivers and produces 5000 continuous horsepower. Six units were delivered starting in June, 1951, including two Great Northern demonstrators. They incorporate the latest diesel technology and can be MU-ed with the P5a motors. This trio heads east out of Thorndale. (E2B-Ball; all others-Tatnall)

In the early 1900s, President Alexander Cassatt took note of the fact that both the freight traffic and passenger traffic between Philadelphia and Pittsburgh were increasing at dramatic levels. Stockholders at the time were told the Railroad had reached its saturation point in several locations and that a new line would have to be built eastward out of Harrisburg to New Jersey to handle freight traffic. Enola yard and the Low Grade Line were part of a $67 million program to improve the service.

We are standing and listening, waiting for a freight on the Low Grade Line to pass over the high bridge at Downingtown, headed up the P&T for the Trenton Cut-Off.

We can hear it coming, the humming of traction motors, the rumbling crescendo of one hundred freight cars. The sound of the train draws close, and finally reaches the west side of the bridge. We have a modified P5a leading a standard P5a on a slow moving freight. Picture perfect! And soon after the first train has passed, hotshot CG-2 crosses the spans behind two P5as. This is a Chicago-to-Jersey City train with freight forwarder traffic and car float business for the New Haven Railroad. Whenever a modified P5a is available, it is placed on the head end to afford the crew maximum protection in case of a collision. (Tatnall).

At lower left, eastbound train No. 2, the *Pennsylvania Limited* breaks the temporary quiet around Haverford, Pa., roaring through town, steam heat boiler popping off in the process. No. 2 is a third-rate train, carrying a diner, lounge, coaches, sleepers, and hordes of head-end cars. The "touch of class" on this train is the California sleeper off the *California Zephyr*.

At the upper left, we are now 35.2 miles west of Thirtieth Street Station, at Thorndale, Pa., where helpers are added on both eastward and westward Main Line trains to Paoli and Gap, respectively. On this day, Baldwin-Westinghouse experimental ignitron E3b and E2c rectifiers arrive with an eastbound mineral train. They will get an assist from the smoky L1 as far as Paoli.

A decision was made in 1948 not to electrify west to Pittsburgh, but the Railroad still wanted to replace its aging P5a fleet with more powerful, newer electrics. In 1948, James M. Symes, vice president of operations, stated that "the Pennsylvania Railroad has never had a satisfactory electric locomotive design for freight service." President Clement was convinced Symes was right, and within the year asked Westinghouse, Baldwin, and General Electric to come up with designs for a new electric locomotive for freight service. E3b #4995 and E2c #4998, pictured on the right, represent two of the four Baldwin-Westinghouse locomotives. They pack 6000 horsepower through d.c. traction motors, with the a.c. current being converted by 12 ignitron rectifier tubes. The pusher is on the rear of the train's cabin car at right, and the rectifiers are now pouring 185,000 pounds of tractive effort onto the rail, getting their heavy train underway out of Thorndale. (Tatnall)

This meet (above) between the GG1 electrics and the L1 just south of Enola invites some interesting comments and comparisons. Though quite visual to the photographer, by its smoky presence, along with the need for constant servicing, it is even more evident to the accountants in Philadelphia that the steam locomotives are considerably more expensive to operate, repair, and maintain than the electric locomotives. Case in point: the Railroad uses the figure of 10.4 cents per mile for the maintenance and repair on a GG1. The L1 doesn't fare as well, with a figure of 33.3 cents hung around her boiler. To further underscore the difference, an L1s hauled a test train of 2,470 gross tons out of the Meadows yard to Enola in 1942, consuming 71.7 cents of coal per mile in

the process. A P5a on the same tonnage used 56.2 cents worth of electricity per mile, including costs of generation and distribution of the electricity factored in. During this same period, the Railroad was giving GG1s heavy repairs every 350,000 miles while performing the equivalent class repairs on steam every 90,000 miles. The availability rate of both the GG1 and P5a motors was 90 percent, while the rate of steam classes still operating under the wires was 69 percent. To the train watcher/photographer, the accountants can keep their ledgers!

At upper right, a Baldwin BS-6a switcher arrives at Thorndale with a cut of off-line hopper cars in the small hours of the morning. At lower right, the low winter sun catches FF2 motor #5 shoving SP-2 out of Thorndale en route to Green-

wich yard in South Philadelphia. For the bargain-basement price of $220,000, the PRR purchased seven Great Northern class Y1 electrics along with a Y1a for helper service, rebuilding the Y1s into class FF2s and keeping the Y1a for parts. Since all of these big motors had plain bearings, lubricated with waste, they were restricted to helper service. At 30 mph, or lower, they could pull (or push) anything out of town. On several occasions when they subbed for road power, the bearings failed from overheating. Remember, on the Great Northern's Cascade Mountain profile, with its constant curvature, the motors rarely got over the sustained speeds that the Pennsy is accustomed to. (Tatnall; Sweetland collection; Tatnall)

This is one of those moments when history holds its breath; when we witness it momentarily suspended on a stagelike setting. The battle draws near; it will be a time when impending events will give way to honest differences.

Above, it is springtime, 1947. The land is waking up, dreams abound. It is time to enjoy the Company's wares on display. Time to look at the EMD model E7 diesels, fresh from La Grange and, likewise, it is a good time to really ponder the Baldwin-built T1 duplex, still a factor in the minds of Pennsy motive power designers. Both locomotives represent a bright, new future — their rendezvous with destiny begins tomorrow.

At upper left, the late winter sun catches the noisy departure of train #33. *The St. Louisan* out of Harrisburg at 4:33PM, with one of the road's celebrated T1s on the head end. All of the fifty post-war T1s have Belpaire boilers carrying 300 psi steam pressure, poppet valves, roller bearings on all axles and crankpins. All have one-piece cast-steel bed frames with integral cylinders – radical for the Pennsy and essentially (in the minds of its designers) a logical mate to the GG1 west of Harrisburg. At lower left, and in a newer era, tuscan EFP-15 dual-service diesel #9833A leads off the power for train EC-1 to Williamsport at the Enola diesel shop. The first two A-B-A sets, starting with the 9832A, are the only units out of the order for 54 that received the tuscan passenger livery. (Mahan-Ball Collection; Sweetland; Prophet)

It is 1955 and we have a railroad with over 400 through "arranged service" freight trains each day, along with 625 scheduled local freight trains. This doesn't count the 1,000 or so tonnage freights rolling across the System carrying coal and ore! On the passenger side of the Railroad, over 800 trains, from MU's to long-haul streamliners, are on the property. *Immense* doesn't do the Pennsylvania justice!

On this spread, we get a general lay of the land from the west bank of the Susquehanna River at Marysville, Pa., where the action is mind-boggling. At upper left, M1b Mountain #6738 off the Middle Division waits in the foreground while M1a #6721 opens up, coming off the Rockville Bridge with Altoona bound tonnage. The view at lower left shows train No. 54, *The Gotham Limited,* heading its sleepers, coaches, diner, and lounge east across the bridge en route to Harrisburg and New York. Off to the right is Enola yard. At upper right, PG-5 suddenly appears, heading out of Enola, underway to Conway behind an A-B-A set of EF-15as. At lower right, we get an idea of the vastness of Enola, seeing just a glimpse of the eastbound yard, motor storage, fuel racks, roundhouse, and steel car shop. In the foreground, and taken three years later than the three other scenes, an Electro Motive 1750 horsepower ES-17m works the eastbound hump. Enola is considered "the hot spot" on the Railroad where well over 6,000 cars are classified and dispatched daily.

It should be noted that Rockville Bridge's forty-eight seventy-foot arch spans entitle this magnificent bridge to the reputation as the "world's longest stone arch railroad bridge." It was completed on March 30, 1902, and is the third Pennsylvania Railroad bridge that was built across the river at this location. (Ball)

We're standing on the River Road Bridge just west of Enola watching SW-6 coming in from the west. On the point, an M1, all Pennsy, laying down the sand, getting into the yard. She's possessed with the efficient Belpaire firebox and a combustion chamber that contributes to a good steam-making boiler. She has about the cleanest valve gear in the business, plus the multiple bearing crossheads. To the PRR, that small 70-foot grate means one less axle. Who can find fault with anything about her; she has no trouble keeping 125 cars on the run with those 72" drivers. On the PRR, Mountain means flatlander! #6825 was turned out by Baldwin in September 1926. She is simply magnificent! (Tatnall)

It is 1956. Cash is tight and President James M. Symes is pressing the Interstate Commerce Commission for a 15 percent increase in freight rates to meet inflation, buy new cars and locomotives, keep ongoing maintenance, provide competitive wages, and give a better return to stockholders. Forty diesel units and twenty steam locomotives are under lease to the Railroad. Symes makes no bones about the fact that this is a less costly arrangement than fixing up steam power for standby.

At upper left, EC-2 is stretched out along the lovely Rockville Bridge behind an M1 coming into Enola from Williamsport. In the foreground, a train heads west out of Enola where it will enter the Middle Division at *Banks* tower, a distance of under three miles. At lower left, we bring a little meaning to the "Route RDG-Harrisburg-PRR" routing so often used by traffic managers, rate clerks, and car tracers. Reading's big T1 Northern #2114 has brought a transfer run with Reading interchange traffic from Allentown over to Rockville from the nearby Rutherford yard. The cabin car on the left belongs to a transfer run to Enola. Above, and across the river at Enola, an I1sa works the eastbound hump, shoving the last cars off an inbound freight. Up in the tower, the operator is watching each car (he calls them cuts) rolling through the retarders every twelve to fifteen seconds. By working from the train's switchlist and eyeing the cars themselves, he will control each car's speed using various air pressures on the steel retarders which grip the flanges and the back of the wheels. Everyone in the yard knows that the maximum coupling speed is 4 mph, and the operator doesn't need to be reminded. (Tatnall)

Coal! You can almost see it in the hills. Its presence is everywhere – in the air, in your nose, on laundry, windowsills, carpets, in hopper cars, along the tracks.

This is a world of coal seams, mine shafts, tipples, company stores, row houses, bleak hills, hazy, dirty skies, air-borne coal dust and smoke, criss-crossing rail lines and power lines. Below the ground are the cutters, drillers, shooters, loaders, mine engineers, track layers – all living out their dangerous work in black holes. There are hard times, strikes, fires, cave-ins, and little money. Coal is for the steel mills, the locomotives, for heating our homes. Somehow, and perhaps in an odd sort of way, these scenes are so typically, beautifully Pennsy.

To the left, an H10 switches the Glen Burn Colliery on the west end of Shamokin, Pa. The locomotive and local yard crew are out of Shamokin and will return with loads from the mine to be picked up by S-391 out of Northumberland. On this page, a single I1sa is beautifully backlit in the last minutes of sunshine heading an eastbound ore train out of Northumberland to Mt. Carmel for the Lehigh Valley Railroad and U.S. Steel. On the rear, two more I1s are shoving for all they're worth. By the time they pass, the sun will be down behind the mountain. (Tatnall)

A dreary, dank, dismal day finds "business as usual" at Weigh Scales, Pa., where coal from the nearby anthracite mines is gathered by local freights and weighed to determine charges to the customer. Each hopper is weighed individually for its gross weight, the clerk subtracting the car's stenciled light weight to determine the load. Since everything is shipped and billed by the ton, this is an important, though seldom seen, operation on the Railroad.

On this page, the I1sa. The robust I1s look like they were designed to play the role of gruff holy terror around the Pennsy system! Whether running, firing them, riding (if that's what you call it) on them, or shoving with them, these grunts are positively brutal on all accounts. We forget that the Pennsylvania tried a 2-8-8-2 from American Locomotive in 1911, and an 0-8-8-0 from Baldwin the following year, neither to the satisfaction of the Railroad. The L1s class 2-8-2 turned out from Juniata was far more satisfactory, but the I1s that was outshopped in 1916 was a gem! It was far more powerful, but used much less steam than the L1s. Five hundred and ninety-eight of the beasts were ultimately built.

So here we have the holy terror of two I1sa's, above, exerting no less than 192,052 pounds of tractive effort through enormous $30\frac{1}{2} \times 32$ inch cylinders with a piston thrust of over 182,000 pounds each, biting the rail with 62-inch drivers, raising hell, moving ore east out of Shamokin toward Mount Carmel. Somehow, the weather fits the occasion. (Ball)

117

At left are two more views along the 27-mile Shamokin Branch from Sunbury to the important Lehigh Valley interchange at Mount Carmel. The line's ruling grade is 1.3 percent and the standard train is 9,000 tons – enough to humble even four I1s. At the upper left, two quite vocal I1sa Decapods make their appearance along the Shamokin Creek, a few miles out of Shamokin. As always, two more of the brute 2-10-0s are on the rear. At the lower left and in lieu of I1s, a perfect match of AF-15s approach Paxinos, Pa., trying out the tonnage with the slightly lesser amount of continuous tractive effort of 170,000 pounds. At right, one more look at the Elmira branch, watching M1 #6967 blast through Trout Run, Pa., showing off her big ocean-to-ocean 210 F 82A tender in the process.

Below, and in the waning light of a beautiful day, the usual pair of "hippos" do what comes naturally, at Dunning, Pa. (Sweetland, Ball Tatnall, Tatnall)

There is a wonderful satisfaction in being alone in the countryside. It is conducive to letting go, calming down, as the time just passes by. The air is sweet and the sun's warmth refreshing. There is something new to ponder and enjoy every minute as the panorama of nature takes on a new, intimate scale.

Suddenly, the whole tranquil world becomes alarmingly alive with the sound of an approaching train on Pennsylvania's nearby iron. One of the Company's beautiful big M1 Mountains quickly booms onto the stage, heading Altoona to Elmira (Southport yard) symbol RA-14. The 32-volt headlight on the M1 hardly shows on this bright day, but someone at the roundhouse obviously put some "TLC" into that bright keystone. This is the beautiful Elmira branch near Troy, Pa., on the line out of Newberry. Oddly enough, New York Central also has a parallel line out of Newberry Jct. to Corning, N.Y., one of the few north-south competitive routes. Unlike Pennsy's line, the Central's Pennsylvania Division passes through a spectacular gorge aptly called "The Grand Canyon of Pennsylvania." Below, the rear end of this same train is pictured a few miles north, nearing the New York state line at Columbia Crossroads, Pa.

Both the M1 and the lead I1sa shoving on the N5B carry identical 16-wheel 210 F 82B tenders. In Pennsy lingo, the "210" is the number of gallons of water in hundreds; the "F" designates freight (no steam heat or signal lines); and the "82" the deck height in inches. The "B" indicates a modification. Once explained, it all makes sense. (Tatnall)

1955 was not a good year for the PRR and President James Symes underscored the fact by stating that normally the Railroad replaces 50,000 tons of rail in its ongoing maintenance, but in 1955 the railroad only replaced 6200 tons of rail. Traffic is surging in 1956, however, and the railroad has found it is cheaper to lease than to fix up. Four hundred tons of evidence is offered in the form of leased Reading T-1 class Northern #2113, above, ready to leave Northumberland, with a job out of Enola to the New York Central interchange at Newberry Jct. One PRR engineman summed up the general feelings about the big 4-8-4s when he said, "The Reading engines are easy at starting a train." At upper right, local E-7 out of Northumberland approaches the Shipper's Car Line tank car repair plant at Milton, Pa., with cars "home for repair." This is a 660 horsepower BS-6a. As if to add to the traffic lull problems of 1955, Hurricane Diane lashed the eastern states on August

7th with frightful fury and continuing rains of such ferocity that the strongest man-made barriers to Mother Nature were rendered almost useless. The terrific storm took 184 lives and wreaked heavy rains for over twenty days. When the skies finally cleared, it soon was apparent that this storm had caused more damage than any other series of storms on record in America. At middle right, Erie GP-7s displaced by washouts on their line come off the bridge across the Susquehanna River at Williamsport, Pa. and are about to cross the Reading at *WG* tower. They will continue along the Pennsy to *Newberry* tower where they will head up the Elmira Branch to rejoin Erie rails at Elmira, N.Y. Below, some more displaced visitors from hurricane washouts. This time three DL&W FT diesels with a freight out of Buffalo, pictured coming off the Elmira Branch at Newberry Jct., about to head onto the Susquehanna Division and down to Northumberland, where they will rejoin home rails over to Scranton. The caboose on the head end is for engine crews on this circuitous routing. Most of the flood damage on the Erie and Lackawanna Railroads is from the rampaging Chermung River between Elmira and Binghamton. At left, one of Pennsy's unique cast iron grade crossing signs up along the Elmira Branch (Sweetland; Ball; Ball; Di Censo; Di Censo)

Sunrise, and we have war freight, westward bound. Four thousand miles to the east, Allied forces are crossing the Rhine River in pursuit of the Nazi forces. Not since 1805, when Napoleon crossed the Rhine, have invading forces repeated the feat. The battle of the Rhineland has been raging and the U.S. Ninth Army and the First Army have been driving toward Cologne and Remagen, while the Third Army has been striking toward Goblenz. The beleaguered Germans are being pushed across the Rhine and for the Allies, the destruction of the heart of the Ruhr is now the final objective to the ultimate smashing of Hitler's Germany. In the Pacific, MacArthur's forces are mopping up the Philippines and the Marines have captured Iwo Jima. We can now give our B-29s, based in the Marianas, fighter cover enroute to Japan, as well as emergency landing fields. The rushing M1a is pictured in early spring of 1945, at Huntingdon, Pa., war goods in tow, bound for West Coast ports. (Cope)

Above, and a few months later, Berlin has fallen on May 2, 1945, just 48 hours after it was reported that Hitler had committed suicide. On May 7, 1945, at 2:41AM, a totally defeated Germany formally surrendered to the Allies at General Eisenhower's headquarters in Rheims, France. The fighting continues in the Pacific, however, with full preparation for the invasion of Japan. There is a lot of talk about ending the war, and as evidence, there is much talk about industrial demobilization in the U.S. In April, the U.S. Army cut its program for small arms ammunition and the Navy has canceled plans for building 72 vessels as part of an "insurance fleet." The Pennsylvania and many other railroads have started to rebuild their war-torn roadbeds, as evidenced in this view along the four track main at Warrior Ridge, Pa. Pride on the Railroad runs deep – from subsoil and cinders, up through 18 inches of well-trimmed ballast, to the crossties, and heavy rails. (Cope)

Some more Middle Division vignettes. Being quite partial to the Pennsy's fabulous Mountains, I gladly take this moment for us to look at another one of these fine machines, at left, moving a westbound empty hopper train near Mapleton, Pa. By the looks of things, the fireman is earning his pay. Below the M1a, four of Baldwin's big BP-20 passenger A and B shark sets have been de-rated and re-geared for freight service into BF-16z classifications. One of the handsome units teams up with an RF-16 and an RF-15, urging Enola to Detroit hotshot ED-3 through the curves and universal interlocking layout at Huntingdon, Pa.

At upper right, a serene look at the track troughs (sometimes called track tanks; and on other railroads, track pans) at Mapleton for picking up engine water on the fly. The trough is centered between the rails and is usually about eight inches deep and nineteen inches wide. A white target and/or lunar light marks the entrance for engine crews to lower the scoops. Many a time, poor unsuspecting hobos had their first encounters with these troughs while riding on the tender beam. Frequently these poor souls who traveled in the winter were found frozen to death at the end of the run. As for the water in the troughs, there is a steam heat plant at each trough location to supply live steam directly into the water to keep *it* from freezing. The Mapleton boiler house is in the background. At lower right, a westbound 4-8-2 with the newer generator and headlight arrangement, but with slot pilot and footboards, hot foots it down the long tangent track through Mt. Union, Pa. (Ball; Lloyd; Prophet; Van Dusen, Ball Collection)

On the following spread, another look at the M1 – never too much of a good thing. After the Blue Ribbon Fleet has passed throughout the night, the heavy steel rails of the Middle Division largely belong to the M class engines and the trains they pull. Whether rolling Pullmans at eighty, hauling coal, or highballing merchandise, these fabulous dual-service machines have the respect of the Railroad. Clockwise from top left, M1-powered trains at Duncannon, Forge, and over the Juniata River near Duncannon, all westbound. If any one picture in this book sums up what the Pennsylvania Railroad is all about, the Juniata-built M1a blasting through Forge is it. (Cohen; Harley; Ball)

127

They come. *And they come!* Like a swarm of locusts, diesels from Fairbanks-Morse, Baldwin, EMD, Alco, and Lima are settling on the property. And they keep coming, dressed in Brunswick and gold, adorning keystones. Many steamers have fallen, and there is no end in sight. It is June 1951, and we are at trackside at Union Furnace, Pa. The realization of the statement in last year's annual report that the Railroad's investment in diesels had surpassed electrification as the road's most expensive single investment, hits hard.

At the upper left, 6000 horsepower worth of Fairbanks-Morse steam generator-equipped Erie Builts, accompanied by a blaring air horn, roar under the signals, highballing eastbound train No. 72, *The Juniata,* from Pittsburgh toward New York. Above, and at the lower right, the rear end of *The Juniata* disappears behind fast-approaching PG-1 and its brand new EMD model EF-15a diesels. The going away shot of PG-1, at left, completes the action. It is obvious the sphere of influence the T1s and Q2s have had on the Railroad has been made precarious by a society of look alike diesels with a stunning mobility to roam systemwide. Back east, the very first class E2b electrics from General Electric have arrived on the Railroad, also dressed in Brunswick and gold, adorning keystones. (Harley)

It is 1951, and the anguishing news to a lot of us is President Truman's removal of General MacArthur from all of his commands. On the home front, manufacturers have been putting more goods into the marketplace than consumers are taking out. Traffic is down on the financially strained PRR and, perhaps, more anguishing than the ongoing Korean conflict without MacArthur is what we see here in East Altoona.

The unrelenting diesels are starting to have their negative effect on the ranks of steam, and the modest downturn in traffic isn't helping matters. Though usually not discussed, Pennsy policy is to keep the shop forces occupied in case of an upturn in traffic. Talk coming out of Washington is for the country to be prepared just in case, and by the looks of things the Railroad is doing just that. At upper left, K4sa #5481 heads the line of freshly shopped locomotives. All around us, the thunder of the silence is deafening among the ranks of dead steamers. Standard shop practice is to paint the tender decks with red oxide; the older locomotives are given red oxide cab roofs. All of the modern locomotives after the M1as get Brunswick green. Note the production T1s have oval-shaped single stacks in lieu of the double stacks that the two prototypes have. And note the T1s even get the insides of their stacks painted red oxide! Modelers, are you paying attention? On this page, more of the dearth, looking back toward the coal wharf. M1b #6774 is the last 4-8-2 built by the Pennsy – outshopped by Juniata in November 1930, bearing construction number 4248. She sits silent, waiting for her call. At lower right, more of the silence. (Harley)

133

By 1900, the railroads were thoroughly converted from wood to coal, and in that year a whopping 212 million tons of bituminous coal came out of the mines in Pennsylvania, Ohio, West Virginia, and Illinois, a good deal of it passing in and out of Altoona.

This spread *is* the Pennsylvania Railroad! The view across the page is from Slayman Avenue, looking toward East Juniata and the eastbound classification yard. The loaded hoppers have been weighed at Altoona and will be headed east to Enola. The BWCX "black ball" GLA hopper identifies the cut as originating in the Cresson, coal area. At left, we are looking off Route 22 at an L1 switching a cut of cars into the Hollidaysburg yard. The line east, behind the tender, comes off the main at *Pete* Interlocking near Petersburg. At the immediate right is a wondrous view of the East Altoona engine house complex. This spread of the PRR at work may be my favorite in the book. (Ball; Cohen; Cohen)

Company Town. Altoona, where it is said you cannot tell if it is spring or fall since the leaves on the trees are always black. And in nearby Juniata, downwind, it is said that *nothing* grows except cinders! At the upper left, we are looking east from the Eighth Street Juniata Bridge (known to PRR employees as "Red Bridge") toward the eastbound classification yard and specifically an I1 cutting off a string of classified cars. The eastbound rip track and MofW tracks are seen in the distance over on the left. At the immediate left, is Second Avenue, Juniata, and the houses that locals say were built three-fourths with stuff from the Company shops – houses, it is said, that lean toward the track everytime a train passes! More to our center of interest, are the helper layover tracks and the BH-50 and EH-15 helpers. The yellow stripe on the door connotes that these engines are exclusively in helper service. The EH-15s were built as helpers in LaGrange and were delivered with the stripe, right to these tracks! Above, we are looking the other way off Red Bridge toward East Altoona, I1sa #4472 switches the east end of the westbound classification yard. In the background are box cars out of heavy repair from the PRR's Samuel Rea shop, moving through the eastbound classification yard. Up in town, all porches are washed every morning, and the curtains, once a month! (Cohen; Cohen; Ball)

At the upper left, we watch No. 24 with its heavy array of head-end cars passing the westbound home signal for *Hunt* Interlocking at Huntingdon, Pa., east of Altoona. *Hunt* Interlocking is unusual in that its plant is right through the station. We are at its easterly limits where we can see the signals that govern westbound trains. The lunar white lights are train order lights. Just west of the station, the 52-mile Huntingdon and Broad Top Mountain Railroad has its passenger connection with the PRR. At lower left, the last A-B-A set of Fairbanks-Morse "C" Line class FF-16 diesels delivered to the Railroad moves through Altoona past Passenger Shop #1. This is 1951, and the shop men are getting ready to start modernizing P-70s for new *Congressional* streamliners. At upper right, and six years later, we have an overall view of the Erecting and Machine Shop, turntable, and radial tracks (known as "the circle" to the shop forces) at Altoona. This is a time of transition on the Railroad and to many railroaders in Altoona who had a part in building the proud steamers. The L1 in the foreground is no longer needed, and is being burned and cut up for scrap. Other steam locomotives are being scrapped in one of the bays inside the E & M Building to keep shop forces busy. Most of the steamers are being "sold on the hoof" to the larger scrap dealers. The Great Northern 259 ton Y1 box cab electric will be rebuilt to a class FF2 motor for use by the Railroad back East. Nearby is Great Northern Y1a motor #5011, which is going to be kept for spare parts. At lower right, a look at Baldwin's beautiful and rugged BF-15 sharknose diesel with its T1-styled nose. She's a bittersweet reminder of the duplex days of the '40s. Oh yes, the railroad opted to go to Budd for brand new cars for the *Congressional* streamliners. All work was halted on the P-70 modernization program for these trains. (Shop scene-Ball; all others-Cohen)

At left, this is the eastern-most end of the yard trackage at Altoona near Bellwood, Pa., where *Bell* tower guards the east end of the westbound receiving yard. The two EFS-17ms sandwiching a "beep," are coming in off the Middle Division with westbound merchandise for Conway Yard in Pittsburgh. (Watching this train, I can almost swear I am looking at two GP-9s and a cabless b-unit geep 9!) At the lower left, Alco AFP-20 class diesel #5759A looks like she has fallen on hard times. The unit is at East Altoona, just off of LA-1 from Lewistown. After refueling, the 2000 horsepower Alco will head back on AL-2. #5759A was built in 1947 as an AP-20, geared for 100 mph passenger service work. She has obviously since been downrated and regeared to dual service status.

There are thirty-six regional shops performing maintenance on the diesels, and unlike the customary strict assignment of steam to particular regions, grand divisions, and enginehouses, diesels maintained by one region may be used anywhere on the Railroad. Each month, every diesel must be returned to its home base for required servicing.

On this page, FAs to an ordinary railroader, AF-15s and AF-16s to a Pennsylvania man. Specifically, AF-15 #9605 heading a mix of 15s and 16s off the Bald Eagle Branch with "the car hauler" transfer run from Tyrone to Altoona, where the hopper cars will be weighed prior to heading on east to Enola. The A-B-B-A powered train is seen at Tyrone. At lower right, a perfect match of AF-16s pass us at trackside, heading a Chicago-bound hotshot through Tipton, Pa. (Sweetland)

On this spread, some diesel-spotting off of Red Bridge in Altoona. To the left, and certainly one of the best angles from which to photograph the straight, honest lines of Alco's FA diesel, an A-B-A set of AF-16s enters Altoona with a Conway job from Enola. In the background, an ES-17m class SD9 road switcher works the old westbound classification yard which was closed in the early 1950s. On this page, an interesting potpourri of six-motored work horses from three of the builders. Clockwise from upper left: a Baldwin BS-16ms, an EMD ES-17m, and a Fairbanks-Morse FS-24m Train Master. This last

view of two of the big 2400 horsepower TMs is at Gallitizin, moments before the engines are going to be cut off at *AR*, after shoving an eastbound mail train up the western slope. It is at times such as this, when we're seemingly inundated with diesels, that we have to remind ourselves that the PRR is a coal road and one that placed high hopes of perfecting coal-burning locomotives. The diesels simply were masters of the game Pennsy wanted to play, and at a lower cost. Their first appearance on the Standard Railroad not only resulted in winning round one, but all of the rounds to come. (Sweetland)

On the lower left, a pair of BS-24 transfer units head west toward Conemaugh yard at Johnstown, where these engines are assigned. We're looking at downtown Altoona from the Ninth Street foot bridge. Above, a "snapper set" of Alco ARS-18as shoves hard against the drawbar on the N8, passing *Slope* tower, headed westward out of Altoona toward the mountain. At right, and 180 degrees in the opposite direction, six EFS-17m haulers head through *Slope*'s interlocking from No. 2 track over to No. 4. It is Company policy not to mix classes of diesel power, even from the same builder. By way of example, EMD GP7s are not to be operated with GP9s. At immediate right, two EMD F3 class EF-15s descend off the Pittsburgh Division with an eastbound mineral train. With only two units, this man doesn't have much dynamic braking and consequently, the smoke. The ARS-18as shove on toward the slope in the distance. (BS-24s-Ball; all others-Sweetland)

This is August 1939, up on the Curve. It seems to be a time of transition across America. The terrible depression is over, but is still on everyone's mind. And there is bewilderment – concerning capital, concerning industry which, in the face of enormous demand, does not produce. Labor seems to be at constant war with itself; and perhaps of most importance, there is bewilderment concerning our government: what is it supposed to do and what is it here for? One thing is a given, that Americans want to enjoy life; it's just a matter of when and how. The daily editorials in newspapers and magazines seem to be asking our government to change from their pessimistic stance of waiting for an emergency to taking an optimistic stance of encouraging growth and bigger business.

Over the last decade, radios have ended up in almost everyone's home; air transport has reached full commercial status; and the automobile has been greatly developed into a comfortable, reliable machine. In newspapers and on radio there are reports of the popular New York World's Fair where inventions including television, nylon, air conditioning, and an aerodynamically-styled locomotive publicly called "the big engine" are on display. The huge locomotive, completed at Altoona this year and rushed to the World's Fair is a streamlined 140-foot long bullet, the largest in the world. It is Altoona's first duplex and is said to be able to handle 1200 tons of varnish at 100 miles per hour. The monster is steaming away at a much slower rate now, however, as it glides on rollers at the Fair.

Now, as we watch these freights on Horseshoe, we wonder if the deeply rooted forces of conventional conservatism on the PRR are going to change on the Railroad. Today we can rejoice in the fact that standard power is at the helm of the trains along the Pennsylvania Railroad. Clockwise from lower left, an I1s works heavy tonnage out of Altoona up No. 3 track right at milepost 242 en route through the apex of the Curve to Pitcairn Yard outside Pittsburgh. At upper left, another I1s drops down No. 1 track at Kittanning Point with a stone train from Conpitt Junction. The white metal target up on the signal bridge with the "G" is a grade signal indicating that freight trains with 50 percent or more of the rated tonnage do not have to stop at a stop-and-proceed signal, but continue at restricted speed (hard to do on a 1.86 percent grade). At upper right, I1s Decapod #4260 handles coal down the mountain and under the semaphores at Kittanning Point, while below, and not far behind, hotshot SW-8 from St. Louis to Enola rolls through the Curve behind M1a #6710. This is the first M class engine equipped with footboards; the 6700 through 6709 are equipped with the slat-type passenger pilots.

Now, as we watch the standard power of the PRR, we do think about that World's Fair engine; more to our understanding, we remember that huge Chicago & North Western E-4 Hudson #4003 that was here October 27, 1938, and the fact that the Railroad was interested enough in her to try her out. Sure, rival New York Central has a masterpiece of a 4-6-4, but it would have been treason to have allowed one on the property, let alone take an admiring look at her, or worse yet, a test run. The Railroad had its taste of 300 psi boiler pressure, four-wheel trailing truck, Baker valve gear, and 84″ drivers with the North Western Hudson. And who knows, the Railroad may have seen a new vision on October 26, 1938 when they put the hugh 4-6-4 to work on the test plant's stationary rack, before it went west for some high-speed runs on the Ft. Wayne Division. For now, the PRR has the world's largest locomotive with a *six*-wheel trailing truck, 84″ drivers, and 300 psi boiler pressure. (Prophet)

It is sunrise on the mountain, and the assault of trains up and down the slope continues. The Blue Ribbon Fleet of Limiteds has passed during the night, but by day, the variety and action is every bit as exciting. Leading the charge are the linebackers from Alco, Baldwin, EMD, and Altoona. Clockwise from upper right, you can always count on Mail No. 13 to appear on the curve around 9:00AM. Today an ES-15 leads three AP-20s. She has a B74 horse express car on the head end today. At lower right, eastbound train No. 72, *The Admiral,* is two hours off schedule. She's heavy on the air, trailing a mix of cars into brakeshoe smoke, including two Rock Island *Golden State Limited* sleepers. Below, a pair of smoky T1s lead the attack on the slope with westbound mail and express No. 95. At left, two members of the 125 fabulous super power J1 class locomotives descend down No. 1 track with a merchandise train. Stay around, the action's only beginning! (Cohen; Prophet; Cohen; Lloyd)

At 12:01 midnight, June 13, 1942, Lieutenant Commander Linder of the German Kriegsmarine brought his sub U202 to surface in the foggy waters off Amagansett, Long Island. Quietly, a rubber raft was deployed with four men and a huge crate of supplies. As the sub slipped away, the four Germans made it to American soil. Shortly after changing to civilian clothes, burying the crate and checking their map, the team of Germans was challenged by a frightened, unarmed U.S. Coast Guardsman. Speaking fluent English, the four said they were fishermen from nearby Southampton. The men caught Long Island Rail Road No. 21 out of Amagansett for Jamaica and New York with $50,000 cash and directions, contacts, and orders printed on their handkerchiefs. First targets were to be nuisance bombs in Penn Station, New York and Philadelphia. Then they were to blow up a Philadelphia aluminum plant and proceed west to blow up interlocking plants on the PRR, and the Gallitzin tunnels. This was Germany's way of recognizing the Pennsylvania Railroad's important role on the home front in the U.S.

Like a giant perpetual motion machine, the great engines of the Pennsylvania Railroad continue their around-the-clock march on the mountain. At lower left, mail No. 9 makes its arousing early morning appearance en route to Chicago behind a GP7 and PAs. Mail No. 9 passes us above, its rider-combine now passing the snapper set of EH-15s at right, on the westward climb. At upper left, the four tracks set the stage for the thundering appearance of a J on westbound merchandise. Her steady, booming, thunderous voice echoing through the nearby hills. (J1-Ball; all others-Cohen)

Since January 1854, the Pennsylvania Railroad's crossing of the Alleghenies has been a classic arena of conflict between mountain and machines, the rails rising 95 feet per mile on the tangents and 85 feet per mile on the curves. The battle westward begins in Altoona and continues for the next 12 miles to the summit at *AR* tower in Gallitzin.

Down in Altoona, the hogger wastes no time getting his train going, knowing he needs a start on the hill and its average 92.4 feet of elevation per mile. Shortly after Brick Yard crossing, the heavy steel rails start to rise at a dramatic angle and the engineers open throttles for the attack. Today the hauler is J1 class locomotive #6423 unassisted on the point. On the rear end are two I1sa "snappers" (Pennsy's slang for helpers) shoving

with everything they've got. This train's tonnage is enough to warrant another J1 on the head end, but with good enginemen and good fires to work with, they should have no trouble.

The engineer on 6423 glances at the steam pressure sitting at 265 pounds, eyes the water glass, and yells over to the fireman, "This is where friendship ceases!" A little further up the Railroad, things get rougher; the hogger is heard to say, "I got the sand under her . . . come to me, baby." He's serious, almost grim. The fireman works the stoker, pays absolute attention to the job. This is teamwork between engineer, fireman, and machine. The engineer feels the hard-working engine through his gloved hands on the throttle and sander valve; he listens to each boom of the stack. Gauges jiggle; water spurts

from pipes on the backhead; the thrust of rods and pistons heaves through the cab.

Up on the Mountain, they pass through the 6° Wilkes Curve. The fireman looks down from the cab at the long shadow of the great engine cast over six ribbons of rail. On the engineer's side the nearby rocks threaten to tumble onto the tracks from the thunderous booming of the stack. "You don't have to shake it. I'll clean it up for you!" yells the engineer. They steadily blast up grade, through the 6° McGrvys Run curve to the left. Shortly, they head into Miller's Curve, 6° back to the right. The big 2-10-4 raises incredible hell through the nearby woods and mountains. Steam is still up around 255 pounds, "with a feather in her cap." She hammers hard into the heavily ballasted 9° curve to the left at Baker's Run. "You put it

in, I'll burn it!" shouts the engineer. The big engine is steady, into a 2°45′ curve to the right, and then around the wall of Kittanning Point. The Railroad can be seen high up on the mountain to the left. Horseshoe's great 9°, 30″ curve comes into view. In a minute, they are into the apex of Horseshoe, "puttin' 300 feet into the air and not a kink in it no place."

"Look her over. See if it's black," the engineer tells the student fireman who is with them today. The great mountainous amphitheatre spreads out ahead and to the left over the reservoir. Eastbound general merchandise is coming down the Railroad, high over Sugar Run. They meet the train headed by members of the largest fleet of Fairbanks-Morse Erie-builts in the U.S. heading down No. 1 track, back toward Altoona. (Tatnall)

On this page, a look at *Hunt* and *Monon* towers on the PRR, both to be considered monuments to the Railroad's early involvement in interlocking plants.

At the upper left, the classic Pennsylvania interlocking tower with its touches of Greek Revival, Italianate, and Renaissance Revival architecture. The bay window, low pitch hip roof, belt course, and quoins tell us it's Pennsy; the keystone identifies the tower as *Hunt,* guarding the interlocking at Huntingdon, Pa. The interlocking machine is a 32-lever US & S electro pneumatic P-3. There is also a 30-lever CTC machine that controls *Deer* at the west end of the Huntingdon icing station, as well as *Pete* at the junction of the Hollidaysburg and Petersburg Secondary. In a sense, *Hunt,* as well an *Monon* and for that matter all of the towers on the Railroad, are standing monuments to automatic railroad interlocking since the first installation of an interlocking plant was on the PRR at East Newark, N.J., in February, 1875. Before the interlocking towers and their control of switches and signals, trains had to stop, look, and listen before crossing over a main track or another railroad's tracks. At lower left is *Monon* tower

at the west end of the Panhandle Bridge on the south side of Pittsburgh. Inside the plain-Jane classic wood tower is a 48-lever GRS model 2 electric machine that controls the wye junction for trains out of Pittsburgh on the Panhandle Main Line, as well as the Monongahela Division up from Brownsville. The Liberty Bridge across the Monongahela River is in the background.

At upper right, Pennsylvania Station in Pittsburgh, completed in 1901, with its unique arched vestibule entrance to the combined terminal and twelve-story office building. At the lower right, the self-explanatory sign by the main entrance to Conway Yard, located twenty-two miles northwest of Pittsburgh along the north shore of the Ohio River. The new $34 million dollar yard replaces an older Conway Yard and is expected to help the Railroad cut east – west freight schedules by up to 24 hours. The eventual plan is to replace many of the 152 existing yards by consolidation into new, larger, more modern facilities such as Conway. (Hunt Tower-Prophet; all others Tatnall)

On this page, Pittsburgh, bastion of America's might, the sweat shop of the nation. The view at immediate left is of the Turtle Creek Valley with the Edgar Thomson Mills and the East Pittsburgh Works of Westinghouse. That's iron ore dust spewing forth from the open hearth furnaces. The four-track main line of the Pennsylvania is prominent, as is the Union Railroad, which crosses in the foreground. President Theodore Roosevelt once said, "There is no more typical American city than Pittsburgh. And Pittsburgh, by its Americanism, gives a lesson to the entire United States. Pittsburgh has not been built by talking about it." Indeed, as the saying goes, "a smoky Pittsburgh is a healthy Pittsburgh." At the lower left, J1a #6500, the last J1a class engine built, rolls merchandise along the mills of Pittsburgh. At upper right, we have a generic view of standard PRR position light signals. They were first introduced into service between West Philadelphia and Paoli on June 24, 1915.

Since enginemen clearly felt they could see yellow signals best, especially in adverse weather, the Railroad standardized them. The PRR was also quick to realize that these signals would be cheaper to maintain than semaphores. Below, an Alco RS-3 class AS-16ms heads a commuter train from Burgettstown into Pittsburgh along the Ohio River in the picturesque West End section of Pittsburgh. (Tatnall; Lloyd; Ball; Holtz)

Paradise for those of us who love big nonarticulated power! The year is 1956, and I speak, of course, of the 112.7 mile Sandusky Branch between Columbus and the lake port at Sandusky: stomping ground for Pennsy 2-10-4s, and since April, twelve enormous Santa Fe 2-10-4s leased to help with an upturn in traffic. In 1946, gross ton miles per freight train hour on the Railroad were 37,150. By 1955, this figure had risen to a healthy 53,205 gross tons. During this same period, average freight train speed on the PRR increased from 13.8 to 17.3 miles per hour, with net tonnage per train rising from 1,339 tons to 1,486 tons. The great J1 locomotives pictured at the left certainly played an important role in boosting these numbers.

At the upper left, and in a power-balancing move, two of the magnificent J class engines head a caboose hop down the Sandusky Branch toward Columbus. They are at milepost 85, about to rattle across the B&O's Akron – Chicago Division at Attica Jct. At lower left, two of the Js throw an incredible 217,500 pounds of tractive effort, some sand, and magnificence, into the job of getting a northbound coal train underway out of Grogan Yard, Columbus. As mentioned in the text, the J1 and J1a class locomotives were built at the outbreak of World War II, patterned after the C&O T-1. The Pennsylvania just didn't have the time to design and build its own freight locomotive under War Production Board restrictions, and as matters worked out, there were no regrets.

On this page are two views of leased Santa 5011 class 2-10-4s on the Sandusky Branch. At the immediate right, Santa Fe's mammoth and majestic 74″ drivered Texas type #5016 moves a seemingly endless train of hoppers over the Nickel Plate iron at Bellevue, Ohio. It is hard to draw parallels between the PRR and Santa Fe; one similarity however, is each railroad's stubborn insistence on using two-cylindered steam power to conquer mountains. At the lower right, a grand portrait of this queen-in-steam, #5022, easing down the rails to grab on to 10,000 tons of coal-laden hoppers for Sandusky.

Pennsy crews affectionately call the mammoth oil burners "the western engines." They are officially classified J1 (o.f.), on the Railroad, indicating the 2-10-4 wheel arrangement and the fact that they are oil-fired. The engines have more difficulty than the J1 starting a heavy train; but once underway, they have more horsepower to really roll. The big problem with the Santa Fe engines is their incredible wheelbase of 109 feet 8 inches and overall length of 123 feet 5 inches. They cannot be turned on the St. Clair Avenue Enginehouse (Columbus) 110-foot turntable. An awkward modification to the turntable, extending the rails out and up 45 degrees over the lead tracks has been made, though it remains difficult to turn the western brutes. Even with this arrangement, the water has to be very low in the tank to keep weight down, and the extension rails from bending. (Ball; Ball; Sweetland; Kring)

An entire chapter couldn't cover the magnificent Cincinnati Union Terminal and the colorful trains that serve the Queen City. The station, completed in 1933, can be seen at upper left, with its 200-foot entrance portal, waiting room and train concourse that spans eight platforms. The trains, from left to right, are Central's *James Whitcomb Riley* for Chicago, Southern's departing *Royal Palm* to Jacksonville, Pennsy's arriving *Cincinnati Limited* from New York, and L&N's *Pan American,* ready to depart at nine o'clock for New Orleans. At right, a closeup of the *Cincinnati Limited* and the *Pan*. At lower left, Baltimore & Ohio's elegant P-7d streamlined 4-6-2 aptly mirrors the architecture of CUT, laying over on the nearby enginehouse tracks under the Harrison Avenue Viaduct. Below, another look at the Terminal's enginehouse leads, where EMD's products are fetchingly displayed by the NYC, C&O, L&N, and the PRR. (Schultz; Marre; Schultz; Sweetland)

Having controlling interest of another railroad can be handy, especially if you're short of power. Such is the case here with the upsurge of 1956 traffic and the controlling interest in the DT&I. Leased Geep #964 works with a PRR mate on a local south out of Logansport, Ind., on the Indianapolis Main Line toward Frankfort and the Crawfordsville Branch to Terre Haute. At immediate left, an H9s with an N6B cabin car works the yard at Logansport. On the right, it's summertime at Dodson, Ohio, on the D&U fifteen miles west of Dayton. K4s #5413 has a roll on *The Union* bound for Richmond and Chicago. B&O's local from Union City, Ind., waits patiently in the hole. Once No. 907 clears, the freight heads towards Dayton on the joint PRR/B&O trackage, trailing its I-1 caboose. (Left page—Eudaly; right page—Scholey, Oroszi Collection)

"Okay, Guys, grub out all of the weeds! Dump new ballast over here; spread gravel for pathways along the tracks; get those signs painted and leave room to get the ice in." *Truckloads* of ice, that is. "Remember, one car with an ice-activated air conditioner takes 4500 pounds!"

Derby Day approaches, and the chiefs and big wigs are arriving in town. This is the Portland Avenue yard in Louisville, and the VIP race trains are here from all over. The Fairbanks-Morse FS-20 at left tucks in a tail car. Soon a GS-4 class 44-tonner will move in with a box car full of resister grids for the 120-volt dc-equipped private cars. A portable transformer is on the way for the ac-equipped cars. This is the time to keep the chiefs happy who, in turn, must keep the shippers happy. Why, did anyone say anything about a horse race? Below is the head end power for some of the trains. The Louisville Branch is in the foreground.

"The Js didn't rumble and roar like the M1s – the Js just walked into it. We really had to gun the Ks and Ms, but the Js just took it in stride." (PRR engineman)

On this page, one of those scenes I'd love to just watch. The cold, crisp air of a Hoosier sunset is rudely broken by this savage masterpiece of steam-driven machinery we know as a J1a locomotive. We are 6.9 miles west of Indianapolis Union Station out in farm country across from *Davis* tower where the I&F Branch turns north off "the St. Louis" for Logansport. Down the tracks, #6488 lets no one mistake the fact she's approaching. She has a restricting indication on the westbound high signal east of the tower, and she comes steadily under her exhausting breath. The operator has been hearing #6488 for some time, too, for she has quite a pull up to *Davis*. The journals on the cars are stiff in this cold weather, only adding to 6488's work.

We stand; we shiver; we listen; we watch. The approaching mammoth boils her pillar of warm smoke into the cold, still air. The low sun glints off the keystone but is absorbed by the rest of the dark, cinder-coated engine. The operator now comes down out of his two-story wooden tower with the familiar order hoop. The great 2-10-4 is upon us; for one thundering instant, we witness the orchestration of super power out in the unforgiving temperature of winter. After the long train passed, the operator headed for the warmth of his tower. "Davis extra six four eight eight west on the I&F by at 1642." In a minute, the operator will start throwing some of the levers in the tower, lining up the St. Louis main. The interlocking machine is a 40-lever Saxby & Farmer. (Tatnall; Baldwin; Ball)

The grain elevator, stack and tower seem to ripple in the heat over Seymour, Indiana. The drowsy town, countryside, and railroad have yielded to the hot midday sun on this already quiet Sunday afternoon. Even the shrill whistle of a distant meadowlark is subdued and dreamlike. Now, an air horn is heard off to the south interrupting the quiet. Minutes pass and a chime horn is heard to the left, up north, joining in the discordant chorus. Two trains are now clearly heard approaching Seymour from each direction, announcing their arrival over grade crossings on the north and south outskirts of town. First to appear is a big Baldwin chisel-nosed BP-20 diesel creeping up the passing track to my right. It comes to a stop and the crew gets down onto the ground. The two 1000 horsepower engines continue their drumming idle, almost drowning out *The South Wind*'s approach and stop at the old red brick depot. The crew off the local say "Hi," and walk across the dusty road in front of me down by the head end of No. 90's purple Atlantic Coast Line power. Wise cracks are exchanged between train crews, and the Florida-bound streamliner gets the highball. The E8s waste no time getting out of town as the crew off the local returns to head their train into the station. Once both trains are out of town on the single track iron, out of hearing distance, the land will again belong to the crickets, bees, and meadowlarks.

At the lower left, two PRR E8s have a fast roll on No. 90, down the single track Louisville Branch south of Indianapolis. *The South Wind* operates one day north, the next day, south, with the local filling in on the alternating days between Chicago and Louisville. (EuDaly; Baldwin; EuDaly)

On this page, we have returned to the Pennsylvania Railroad during the last summer covered in this look at the Railroad during the 1940s and 1950s. Deferred maintenance is definitely the rule on the Southwestern Division with every effort being made to slash costs and at the same time improve the overall efficiency of the physical plant.

No. 67 finally shows, a headlight under a high noon sky. Three very fine sounding EP-20s rock over the crossovers past *Kraft* tower and its waving operator, heading westward with *The American*, one hour off the schedule. Seeing three units, head end business, and people in the windows is very gratifying; but that sleek TWA 1649 Connie on

final approach into nearby Weir Cook Airport a minute ago reminds me that things in this world are constantly changing. No. 67's last car clatters past and in a few minutes the train will be by *Davis*. *Kraft* is the junction of the 117.8 mile Vincennes Branch. The Indianapolis Union Belt Line also comes into here. A 16-lever Union

Switch & Signal S-8 machine mounted on top of a 16-lever Saxby & Farmer mechanical machine controls the interlocking. The Pennsy tended to augment mechanical levers with electric levers placed above.

A Delta DC-6 is droning overhead on its downwind leg into Weir Cook; I don't want to think of the fact that the train *used to be* the fastest way to St. Louis. Ironically, PRR's subsidiary, Transcontinental Air Transport, inaugurated cross-country rail–air service back on July 7, 1929, using an advance section of *The American* and Santa Fe's *Missionary* along with Ford Tri-Motors to speed up the journey. When a single plane could make the trip, of course, the rail–air service was discontinued; when a single plane could make the coast-to-coast trip nonstop . . .

At the upper right, a Consolidation handles local freight IS-6 down the Louisville Branch to Camp Atterbury and Edinburg, Indiana. There are four veneer plants at Edinburg with quite a bit of traffic in and out of the town. Gons bring in the logs, and box cars bring out the finished products. There is never too much traffic for the class H9 and H10 Consolidations to handle; why, at one time, the PRR used to have over 3300 class H 2-8-0s on the roster! The 2-8-0 was obviously the standard power on the railroad in an earlier era. At lower right, a dazzling showcase of E units head up the southbound *South Wind* at Garfield Park, just out of Indianapolis, en route to Louisville, Montgomery, Jacksonville, and beyond. It is rare to see all three classes of production Es lashed up on a single train. (Baldwin)

At first glance, this spread looks anything but Pennsylvania Railroad. I offer it only out of selfishness, for "Naptown" has always been one of my favorite cities, because of its people, its places, and yes, for its trains.

Indianapolis is one of the largest American cities not on a navigable waterway, but its trains make up for this deficiency, reaching every conceivable direction: north, south, east, and west. There is a curious mixture of conservatism, neighborhood clannishness, God-fearing church people, Ku Kluxers, educators, poor folk, etc. in Indianapolis, that mirrors the various destinations of the trains. The Monon comes into town — certainly Hoosierland's own little railroad. The big New York Central and Pennsylvania Railroads also come to town, arriving and departing in all directions. So too, the B&O, Erie, Illinois Central, and Nickel Plate, representing a cross section of America.

I have gotten off New York Central's train No. 41, *The Knickerbocker,* at upper left, having come from Harmon, N.Y., on the way to DePauw University at Greencastle. SOP is to check my suitcase down in the station and "hang around" long enough to shoot New York Central's train No. 3, *The James Whitcomb Riley,* arriving and departing shortly after 9:00 in the morning. At 10:30 I will catch PRR's No. 3, *The Penn Texas,* to Greencastle, arriving within walking distance of the fraternity house and a much-needed lunch. At lower left, and viewed from Monon's inbound train No. 11, *The Tippicanoe,* from Chicago, we meet Pennsy's No. 66, *The American,* departing behind EFP-15s for Harrisburg and New York. That is *IU* tower on the left with its 111 lever Union Switch & Signal model 14 electro-pneumatic machine that controls the complex interlocking east of the station. At upper right, a member of rival New York Central's tribe of 275 Hudsons is just in from Cincinnati. She is on the streamlined

Riley. Below, PRR's attempt to eliminate the fireman — the GS-4 class 44-ton switcher. Since it weighed less than 90,000 pounds on drivers, the fireman was not needed. The little GEs proved to be inadequate for switching IU, so an attempt was made to MU them, but largely to no avail. Today, #9313 ventures into the station to pick up two cars. (Ball; Baldwin; Ball; EuDaly)

On the left, we picture local train Nos. 95–75, *The Kentuckian*, from Louisville, and No. 90, *The South Wind*, from Chicago, arriving and departing Indianapolis, respectively. Up until recently, we would have been talking about train No. 307 from Louisville (its counterpart being No. 306) and No. 308 from Chicago (its counterpart being No. 307) so the Railroad's renumbering has lessened the chance of confusing one train with the other.

The big Baldwin BP-20 clatters over the great maze of interlocking into the east end of Indianapolis Union Station which is owned and controlled by the Indianapolis Union Railway. *IU* tower, off in the background, controls all of the interlocking on the east side of the station, including the Jeff wye, through its big M-14 machine. The west end of the large station, on the other hand, has never been a part of the pneumatic interlocking plant. All of the switches are hand-thrown manuals even though there is plenty of room on the M-14 machine in the tower. It was simply determined at one time that paying 2 or 3 switchtenders was less expensive than interlocking. At the lower left, the northbound *South Wind* is departing a little behind schedule according to the clock on the corner tower of the 1869 station. ACL and PRR power is operated on a run through mileage balancing basis, between Chicago and Jacksonville.

On one of my early morning arrivals into Naptown on board No. 31, the westbound *Spirit of St. Louis*, we caught up with a J1 out of Hawthorne yard on a caboose

hop. For a few moments, the big J clanked along on a parallel track as we proceeded through *IU* interlocking into the station. With camera in hand and trying not to look *too* conspicuous, I got off the train, told the conductor I'd be right back, and ran beyond the end of the platform and station canopy to take a picture. I sensed a great urgency to photograph the lone J1 and cabin, fearing the end was near. As things turned out, I was right. The J1 is seen at right, heading west toward Terre Haute. The ever present switch tenders can be seen on this end of the station. The large power plant belongs to the Indianapolis Power and Light Company. (They held the J1 for our train and I caught her light at Greencastle after I had gotten off.) Below, Budd-built tavern lounge, observation #50 brings up the rear of New York Central's smart *James Whitcomb Riley* out of Indianapolis. On the head end of the Louisville-bound train is super J-3a Hudson #5447. (EuDaly, Baldwin; Ball; EuDaly)

The Pittsburgh & West Virginia 1600 horsepower AS-616, above, is shown on assignment on the PRR at West Terre Haute, Indiana. The road switcher is on the Green Valley turn where it serves a local coal mine. The unit could not MU with any other P&WV engines and was, therefore, offered on a lease to the Pennsylvania. The Pennsylvania has eleven identical units classified BS-16ms that *can* be MUed.

At the immediate left, and at lower right, the high speed comings and goings of the PRR along the Southwestern Division at Limedale, Indiana. Specifically, an A-B-A set of EF-15s barrels out of the curve from Greencastle and meets the eastbound *Spirit of St. Louis*, raising dust across the Monon diamond at the posted 70 miles per hour. Up on the signal bridge is the westbound home signal governing train movements over a pair of double crossovers and the Monon main line. *Limedale* tower can be seen behind the head cars on the *Spirit*; it has a 36-lever

old style GRS machine and, more interesting, one of the very first CTC installations covering the railroad from Bridgeport, to Limedale.

Above, one of the two specially modified SD7 diesels, classified ERS-15ax is pictured on a beautiful day at North Vernon, Indiana, heading a local freight south toward Madison and the nearly 6 percent grade down to the Ohio River. #8588 has a 65:12 gear ratio with the pinion teeth geared directly on the armature shaft for the extra strength needed in this grueling service. The unit is also specially ballasted and is equipped with rail washers. When the H6sb and, later, the H10s steam locomotives handled the severe grade, the rule was to always operate on the east end of their train, facing west, in order to keep the water over the crown sheet in the boiler! This part of the PRR was once the Madison & Indianapolis, the first railroad in Indiana, having started operations in 1838 with a rack system. (EuDaly)

Here we have a potpourri of the Pennsylvania Railroad seemingly "far from home," on the western end. The J1, at the immediate left, is hot-footing merchandise through the graceful curve at Caseyville, Ill., east of Effingham. She will go as far as Rose Lake Yard in East St. Louis, Illinois. Below, and 1,050 miles from the platforms at Penn Station in New York, is the throat into St. Louis Union Station. Tower No. 1 at the left, controls the terminal's labyrinth of trackage in and out of the station. Wabash Rail-

road's *Detroit Limited* is seen behind one of the road's smart P1 class Hudsons converted from a K4 (Wabash, that is!) class Mikado. B&O, Pennsy, and GM&O road power can be seen in the background along with a Terminal Railroad Association of St. Louis (TRRA) Alco switcher. The front end of a Missouri Pacific MT-75 mountain is at the right. This class is widely considered to be the fastest 4-8-2s in the U.S. At lower left, two EP-20s head to the 14th Street engine servicing facility. Note the number of double-slip switches in just this view! There's an old saying, "no train ever passes through St. Louis," as all trains end up backing into and departing out of the same station.

In 1869 the lease of the Pittsburgh, Fort Wayne & Chicago Railroad was consummated with the PRR obtaining half of the shares of the Indianapolis & St. Louis Railroad Company and its trackage from Indianapolis to Terre Haute. The Railroad already had a majority of the St. Louis, Vandalia & Terre Haute and, thus, the direct route to St. Louis. As a matter of interest, the Pennsylvania Railroad system is made up of over 400 predecessor railroad companies. At right, and viewed from *HN* tower at North Judson, Ind. K4s #1330 is about to bang across the Erie diamonds with No. 208, *The Union*, from Chicago. The train has come down the Panhandle (formerly the Pittsburgh, Cincinnati, Chicago and St. Louis Railroad Company), and is heading for Logansport, Richmond, and Cincinnati. That's the C&O to Peru and Cincinnati on the other side of the highway. Off to the left, the Erie main to Chicago from Marion and the east. Just ahead of #1330 (on the other side of the tower), the New York Central diamond and the line to Kankakee. At immediate right, the westbound *Spirit of St. Louis* clatters across the Illinois Central main at Effingham, Ill. The 81-lever S&F mechanical interlocking tower belongs to the IC. The "Indianapolis Star" up in 5863's window belongs to the engineer! (Ball; Collection; Ball; Collection; Ball)

Calendar girl – all 1,000,000 plus pounds of her – rumbles and shakes the B&O and Nickel Plate diamonds at Lima, Ohio, rolling the high cars toward Chicago. This is the darling of the duplexes, the great Q2 locomotive outshopped by Altoona in June of 1944. Twenty-five of these powerhouses were built at Altoona with the first of the order rolling out of the erecting bay just before D-Day. To me, she looks like the product of a proud nation with the enormous power and expectation of victory! Once this most powerful of 10-drivered engines passes with her train, we'll take a walk down to *Lima* tower to say hello to the op. and see the 8-lever S&F mechanical and 8-lever US&S S-8 electric machines that control the busy crossing.

At the upper right, local freight LD-21 from Logansport and Plymouth burbles over the Chippewa Road crossing at South Bend, Indiana. Power for the little train comes in a big package today – a 2500 horsepower Lima center cab LS-25. This transfer engine was built in 1950 and was originally offered as a 2400 horsepower unit since its two Hamilton T89S5A diesel engines are rated at 1200 horsepower each. Pennsy insisted on a 2500 horsepower unit, so Lima had to crank in fifty additional horses on each end! At the lower right, a pair of tuscan EP-20s rattle over the Ft. Wayne Division diamond at *P* tower in Plymouth with a train of fighting Irish fans coming up the South Bend Branch to see Notre Dame play football. The milepost marks exactly 159 miles to Terre Haute.

Getting back to the LS-25 – and to the Q2 – there is a poignant recognition of both locomotive classes that should be made. LS-25 #5683, delivered to the PRR in Columbus on September 11, 1951, was the last diesel Lima built. She represented (sadly) the best product available at the time from the genius locomotive builder. So, too, the Q2 class 4-4-6-4 represented Altoona's "best product available" at the time, with Altoona closing doors in June 1946, after the last T1 was built. Even the Q2's unheard of horsepower (almost 8000) could be matched, simply by adding on more diesel units. (Thompson; right page-Van Dusen, Ball Collection)

What dreams are made of . . .

Three factors came into play which resulted in the incredible T1 duplex design: the awesome speed and power of the 1937 designed S1 duplex #6100: the need to run at the Century mark with 1200-ton passenger trains (eliminating double-headed K4s); and the resultant success of K4s class engines modified with rotary poppet valve gear.

A fourth factor, though generally not alluded to, may have been the repugnancy of coal-hauling, coal-burning Pennsy to consider the inroads being made by diesel electrics.

The T1 duplex is basically a smaller version of the S1, designed to do what the huge S1 cannot do – get east of Crestline into Harrisburg. With the combination of divided drive and rigid frame, the T1 is designed to attain high speed with smaller and lighter machinery parts that will reduce wear and tear. Lateral motion devices have been applied to the first and third set of drivers to ease the big locomotive into curves. And unlike four-cylindered articulated locomotives, the T1's rigid frame eliminates maintenance of a jointed articulation connection while permitting better balancing and suspension of her huge boiler.

Prototype T1 locomotives #6110 and #6111 were built by Baldwin and were delivered as experimental locomotives to the Pennsylvania Railroad on April 22, 1942, and May 21, 1942. (Harley)

In 1945 and 1946, fifty more of the exotic Loewy styled T1s were built by Altoona and Baldwin, with Altoona building all fifty tenders. In May, 1946, Ralph P. Johnson, Baldwin's Chief Engineer, addressing the New York Railway Club, gave an account of the new T1 fleet, boasting, "These locomotives will outperform a 5400 horsepower diesel locomotive at all speeds above twenty-six miles per hour, and if given comparable facilities for servicing and maintenance, will do the work more cheaply."

So here we have the great T1, two months after Mr. Johnson's remarks, scooping water on the fly into its titanic tank at the Davis track troughs near Hanna, Indiana, at milepost 404.6. The train is No. 22, *The Manhattan Limited*, eastbound out of Chicago. Though these pictures suggest high speed, the Railroad's tenders are not equipped with the overflow system developed and used by rival New York Central. Consequently, water can not be scooped at the normal track speed. A yellow target marks the exit from the trough, at which time the scoop has to be up. In a very short time, the T1 will have her train back up to track speed, a far cry from stopping at a water plug! (Harley)

In November 1941, President Roosevelt, noting the action of German U-boats against our marine shipping, talked tough to the American people. "The shooting has started . . . America has been attacked . . . We do not propose to take this lying down . . . . Very simply and bluntly, we are pledged to pull our own oars in the destruction of Hitler."

The mightiest industrial effort this world has ever known is now underway throughout America. The all-out effort to meet Hitler head on, on his court, has begun, with war production lines going onto 24 hour schedules. The story is the same for tanks, aircraft, guns, munitions, and anything else Uncle Sam needs. Long lines of enlistees are in the streets. It is said workers are going through doors in the morning that aren't there in the afternoon, as American factories are gutted and re-tooled for military use.

On this spread are some of the war trains along the Pennsylvania Railroad rushing through northern Indiana in unprecedented numbers answering to Uncle Sam's demands.

At upper left No. 71, *The Admiral*, scorches the ballast through Hobart on its overnight run from New York to Chicago behind one of the Company's magnificent K4s locomotives. This remarkable locomotive, with its large, free-steaming boiler, powerful 27 by 28 inch cylinders, and formidable 3500 horsepower, has no trouble keeping up speed – especially with lightweight cars and 80-inch drivers. At far left, an M1 heads merchandise westward about to duck under the EJ&E tracks near Gary. The B&O, Wabash, and New York Central all parallel the Pennsy at this point. Above, eastbound CG-2 with business for car floats out of Greenville, New Jersey, to the New Haven, BEDT, New York Dock and, I suspect, the Brooklyn Naval Yard, blasts under the South Shore's track west of Gary. At left, the L1 has westbound gons in her knuckled grip for use in the steel mills. (Harley)

1942 wears on and we are into Spring. Our GIs are fighting around the world and there seems to be one disastrous setback after another. Talks of victories turn to tales of defeat. Of one thing we are confident – really sure of – and that is the fact that our home front arsenal of democracy is a juggernaut that is *going* to win the war! From factory worker to railroader, air raid warden to community scrap committee head, we're all in this thing together. Farmboys, cowboys, cityboys are shoulder to shoulder, on both fronts giving it all they've got. "The difficult we'll do right now/The impossible will take a little time."

Above, and certainly no stranger to these parts, class N2sa #7939 works a long train of scrap steel up the Panhandle near Schererville, Indiana. We must not forget that steel mills buy tremendous quantities of scrap steel. An open-hearth furnace uses about fifty percent or more of scrap in the making of steel and, of course, the electric furnaces use only scrap. Discarded steel from the mills themselves comes from the constant trimming, boring, and cropping, and will be used again and again. This kind of scrap is called "run-around," and is often shipped from one mill to another in an effort to keep up balanced production. The 2-10-2 has white wash

on its main rod, eccentric crank and valve motion from a recent shopping. This is done to detect possible cracks where oil would seep through. She is sort of an illegitimate child on the PRR system since she is not a standard Company design but a Lines West design out of the Fort Wayne shops. With approval from Philadelphia, mechanical engineers at the Fort Wayne Shops worked up their own class N1s drag engine design for Lines West around the lakeport terminals where slow speed power was needed to lug iron ore and coal. They have a slightly larger grate area than the I1 but carry only 215 pounds of pressure. Absolute top

"speed" is 30 miles per hour. At the time of the order, two separate engineering departments at Fort Wayne and Altoona were maintained for Lines West and Lines East motive power.

Alco and Baldwin quickly built the first of these engines in 1918, followed by sixty N2s class engines of standard USRA design in 1919. The N2s engines were delivered with radial stay boilers which Altoona rebuilt into their standard Belpaire in subsequent years.

More of an attention getter than the N2sa is the colossal S1 duplex at upper right, seen heading *The General* at tremendous speed eastward out of Chicago. She has lost

some of her skirting since returning from the New York World's Fair, in an effort to reduce servicing time. She has *not* lost her ability to run, as evidenced here. Why, just last month, she roared through Plymouth, Ind., with ninety freight cars at 73 miles per hour! A local law officer took to the parallel highway to confirm suspicion and the mayor of the town called Philadelphia! Engineer of tests, Lloyd "L. B." Jones, was onboard enjoying the Pullman-like ride – until arrival in Fort Wayne! At immediate right, and closer than a grand stand seat (perhaps I should say grand *stand*), a between-the-rails shot is offered of the eastbound *Broadway* and *Century* racing through the 4-vertical lift bridge over the Calumet River east of Englewood at River Branch. New York Central's first E7 diesels from LaGrange head the *Century*, a T1 opens up with the *Broadway*, ready to show the diesels a thing or to. Whew! (Harley)

Here is the constant tidal wave of war trains in and out of Chicago: servicemen off to training camps; others coming home on furlough; the main (troop) trains and the regular passenger trains – all filled with more GIs and businessmen. The country is in an unprecedented rush. The tireless K4s is seen in her rolls, wheeling varnish and main trains around the clock. At upper left, hurrying westward through South Chicago; at lower right, eastward through Englewood. The increase of trains means more races along the parallel tracks with rival New York Central. The K4s below has "lost" to the J-3a Hudson at Whiting, Ind., due to the speed restriction at Colehour. At the upper right, there really isn't a contest this time since a G5 is subbing for a K4 today on *The Union*. The G5 is perfectly capable of running 80 with the lighter consist of *The Union*, once underway. She'll go the 109.6 miles to Logansport where a K4s will take over. (Harley)

The world's mightiest industrial complex continues to be fueled by the railroads, as more and more GIs are rushed to points of embarcation. There are over 5,000,000 GIs around the world now in 1943. Uncle Sam needs 5,000,000 additional women to join the war effort at home on assembly lines, as crane operators, molder's helpers, engine wipers, you name it. "Goodby, Momma, I'm off to Yokohama," goes the hit song, and at local movie theaters, Bugs Bunny is singing, "Buy war bonds and invest in the U.S.A." Typical of this year's movies are *Standby for Action, So Proudly We Hail,* and *The Saga of a Lost Patrol.* Tops on the music charts is Glenn Miller's "Dearly

Beloved" sung by Skip Nelson.

Newsreels of Rommel's 10th and 21st Panzer Divisions breaking through our lines in the North African Desert have unified our efforts at home to produce even more. On March 20, Montgomery started to finally push Rommel's troops along the Mareth Line. General Patton bragged, "We're not holding Rommel, we're advancing!" when asked how things were going. The bitterly fought conquest of Hill 609 in Tunisia rallied our spirits at home and restored American prestige on the battlefield. A commanding officer at Hill 609 proudly said, "The American tax payer will take this hill." On May 3, our 1st Armored Division entered Mateur on

the last lap toward driving the Axis forces clear off the African continent. In July, we invaded and took Sicily while Admiral Nimitz was starting to nullify the Japanese advances in their own backyard. MacArthur was planning his campaign to the Philippines. Never before has it been so clear that our GIs are engaged in warfare on a front that stretches around the world. And for the first time, a glimmer of victory is glowing throughout the nation. The song, "Praise the Lord and Pass the Ammunition," is constantly played on the radio, as workers go from sixty hour weeks to seventy and eighty hour weeks. Victory gardens, tin drives, rubber drives, paper drives,

silk stocking drives, and bacon grease drives make everyone feel they're in the war; gas rationing, food rationing, and blackouts make everyone *know* they're in the war. And if there are any doubts about the pace on the homefront, take a look at trackside, at the unbelievable number of trains beating down the cold, steel warpath. Above, an M1a moves part of a division of GIs east, while, at lower right, a year-old J1 heads east, meeting an inbound passenger train. All action is near Englewood. At upper right, another train of GIs heads to war — its rider's names chalked on the cars. (Harley)

War babies. On this bright, sunny day in 1944, two trains stride past our trackside location between the parallel New York Central and Pennsylvania main lines just east of Englewood. These locomotives are the first class citizens of the two rivals: the L-4a suggestively rolling by with a swaggering bravado; the heavyweight J1 rumbling past with the confidence of victor. Both engines function efficiently and unglamorously. Both engines were outshopped in 1943, and rep-

resent the needs of each road's characteristics. And this just may be the most graphic illustration of how *different* the two rival railroads really are! The Lima-built L-4a Mohawk is a dual service machine handling both freight and passenger service. She can handle tonnage and she can keep the *Century* on its schedule. She has 72″ drivers and works with 60,000 lbs. tractive effort. The J1 has 70″ drivers and works with 93,700 lbs. tractive effort without booster. Un-

like the relatively fast L-4, the J will work at 50, or even 60, lugging 150 freight cars on her drawbar. More important, perhaps, she will get down on her hands and knees and walk tonnage up a mountain. The Mohawk's real estate is all on relatively flat ground, "the Water Level Route," if you will. Anything adorning a keystone on the other hand, is going to encounter mountains (and we remember that a Mountain is a Mohawk on the Central!). Each rival claims it is the

fastest between New York and Chicago. On the Central, that's 960.7 miles of railroad; on Pennsy, 907.7 miles. The mountains make the difference.

Aside from the frequency of the trains, there are plenty of other reminders that we are at war. One of the most obvious is the military tone of the advertisements in the papers and magazines. "At ease . . . for refreshment," says Coca-Cola; "America must be first in the air!" states Goodyear; and "Call out

the Reserves!" shouts Pyro Anti-Freeze, showing a bus stalled in wintertime. The automobile ads tell us how to make our cars last; the manufacturers of rubber tell us how to make our tires last. Columbia bicycles advertises the fact the Army and Navy are using their bikes and that defense workers and civilians should use them too, in our effort to conserve. Kayser's new rayon stockings replacing needed nylon are called Victoray stockings. Newspaper headlines and stories

are all war, and magazine covers and even comic books feature war. Superman holds a huge red cross under one arm and reminds us to give generously to the American Red Cross. The Consumer Division of the Office of Price Administration has sent households diplomas that call for "The Consumer's Pledge for Total Defense," reminding people to "buy carefully, take care of what we have," and "to waste nothing." Posters tell us to buy War Bonds, to enlist now, and

to take our place in Civil Defense. There are signs everywhere around the railroad reminding people that "Loose lips can sink ships." A poster on the roundhouse bulletin board at 59th Street shows a GI drowning in the oily sea. It bears the message, "Someone talked!." An American flag adorns the crew dispatcher's wall over at the 55th Street roundhouse with a large "Keep 'em rolling for Victory" sign. AAR posters are everywhere, asking that railroaders guard the sup-

ply lines (the railroads) with an order, "Railroad Men – Alert! Head clear. Eyes open. Mouth Shut."

And, of course, everywhere are updated rolls showing how many PRR men have entered the Armed Forces – and how many have given their lives for their country. Also not easily ignored nor forgotten are the soldiers carrying M-1 rifles, guarding the railroad yards, bridges, and nearby mills. (Harley)

It's 1945 and our fighting tactics are changing as we advance on the European and Pacific fronts. Our confidence on the home front of impending victory swells as we receive news of battles being won in ever-increasing numbers. By late 1943, American war strategists felt something more than the massive bombing of some German factories, transport systems, and multiplying Nazi burdens was needed to end the war. The decision was made to try daylight precision bombing deep inside Germany to hit the very sources of supplies needed for Hitler to build his war-making machines.

By 1945, our B-17s have come close to perfecting the destruction of small industries vital to Germany military production and depriving their armed forces of the means to resist. The most important targets are German bearings of all kinds – ball, roller, tapered, barrel, and so on – that are needed in every weapon, plane, sub, truck, and locomotive. Recent reports have indicated that our bombing has cut back Germany's production of war weapons by up to 45 percent.

The unbelievable high level of business continues along the Pennsylvania Railroad with no let up in sight. Figures show that the Company handled more volume last year than at any other time in its history. The net income was a healthy $64,720,431 with revenue ton miles up to a staggering 68,842,263,599! Passenger miles were an additional 14,920,272,649. These are numbers undreamed of, but they illustrate the incredible war-making capacity of the United States and the Pennsylvania Railroad's role as supply line for Uncle Sam.

Rumors abound that the Company is still thinking about electrifying westward beyond Enola; that President Clement has designers working on two super versions of the GG1 electric – giants that would develop more power than one, or even two J1s! There is all sorts of scuttlebutt around the Railroad that when the war ends, a huge new coal generating power plant is going to be built next to the main line of the Pittsburgh Division, somewhere near Wilmore, Pennsylvania. The fact that *any* train that is passing us here, on these two pages, can be handled by GG1s back east takes on a fresher, deeper meaning. Is it possible the wires will get to Crestline? What if . . .

At the upper left, the M1a rushing past us has dropped her train at Colehour Yard and is heading to the 55th Street roundhouse where she will be serviced and run back east. At the lower left, the eastbound *General* roars through South Chicago behind double-slotted K4s locomotives. Partially de-streamlined K4s #3768 which was assigned to the Loewy streamlined 1938 *Broadway Limited* is on the point.

On this page are two more views taken at Englewood in late afternoon. At upper right, the Company's new S2 steam turbine #6200 punches steam through its four stacks, working the wartime consist of the *Trail Blazer* eastward out of the station. This exotic machine is Altoona's newest creation-in-steam, but enginemen are complaining about her. "She trades water for steam to get going . . . you put the injector on until the water's outa sight – put it back on, and pray!" In truth, recent tests on the constant speed turbine which is connected directly to the drive wheels have showed that steam drops from 310 psi to about 180 psi when starting a train because of the waste of steam powering the turbine at inefficient rotational speeds. The S2 has steam leak problems too, and when you consider the fact that water boiling at 310 psi has a temperature of 424°F and only 389°F at 180 psi, this variance is enough to play havoc on metal. For now, however, she represents the Company's hopes of bettering the diesel-electrics. At right, the trusty duo of two K4s engines gets No. 78, *The Pennsylvanian* underway east out of Englewood Station. (Harley)

We've seen what happened to the once streamlined K4s #3768 in an earlier look. She returned from the World's Fair only to get caught up in the feverish rush of war train assignments. She was part of the railroad industry's fling with aerodynamic streamlining and matching trains that ushered in the Age of Streamlining in the 1930s. In #3768's case, she was Pennsy's point locomotive for the Loewy-styled 1938 *Broadway Limited* that introduced the 142-car "Fleet of

Modernism" to the railroad. The streamlined K4s and its flowing train was a stunning example of the new look of individualism that each major railroad came up with prior to the war. Despite tests that indicated streamlining decreased wind resistance and added horsepower, once the war broke out, shop forces and servicing crews were given the go-ahead to remove enough sheet metal shrouding from the streamlined locomotives to give them quick access for maintenance

during the hectic wartime scheduling. The trains themselves changed too, as once matching cars were mixed up, added onto, and so on, to accommodate the increased demand for seats and sleeping space.

Above, rival New York Central's bid in 1938 was ten stunning Dreyfuss-styled J-3 Hudsons for its new *20th Century Limited*. One time spit and polish #5451, seen streaking, parallel to the Pennsy, westward near Whiting, Ind., with an unstreamlined sister is an example

of what has happened during the war. She has a huge new PT-4 tender, and has lost much of her skirting, as is noticeable here in the unaccustomed role of heading up train No. 35, the *Fast Mail*.

On the right page, we move into the fall of 1945. In the words of a journalist, "The country stands as if on a mountain of power. America has inherited the earth." I like to think of the words of a currently popular song that's so appropriate to our homecoming GIs: ". . . but words can wait 'til another day. Kiss me once and kiss me twice/it's been a long, long time." Signs such as "Welcome Home" and "Bring the Boys Home" are in many windows of houses and apartments along the railroad tracks. In some windows there are signs that simply say, "Victory!"; in many other windows, the tasseled banner hangs, with one or more stars indicating how many men of the home are in the service. At upper right, T1 #5538 is racing past us near 55th Street, about to shut off for the curve and Englewood Station. All of the T1s, save #5500, are equipped with Franklin Type A poppet valve gear. The 5500 had the type B valve gear applied, after she was involved in a side swipe with a K4s in St. Louis. According to the maintenance guys at the Spruce Street Enginehouse (Columbus), the 5500 is "the best of all of 'em since she's easy to work on." The rear unit of a type A is up inside the frame structure and "only accessible to an eight-year-old kid," according to some mechanics. The type B external rotary poppet valve gear applied to K4sa #3847 was a very successful experiment and easy to maintain. It is too bad the Company elected not to use the type B on the rest of the T1s. At lower right, a look at Q2 freight duplex #6178 at 59th Street, resting her nearly 8000 horsepower between runs. (Harley)

In perhaps the loveliest scene in the book, rivals sketch their smoky trails into the pastels of Nature's sunset. It was one hundred years ago that the Pennsylvania Railroad Co. was founded. (Harley)

"I don't know of a case during the war where, if the government needed an item, we couldn't put on enough pressure to get the material to make it, but now . . . ," one plant manager was quoted as saying in 1946.

The abrupt shift from the boom and roar of wartime production to peacetime production is proving to be an exasperating and bedeviling problem. There are basic shortages of raw materials, government con-

trols left over from the war, and problems with labor, from strikes to a what-the-hell apathy on the part of workers. When people talk of "shortages from A to Z," they're talking about shortages from aluminum to zinc which have grievously hurt production. Demand is up, but too many folks seem to want the same things. To quote a Pullman Standard shop man, "There's a catastrophic shortage of screws and a four-year backup on industrial carpeting." An ACF production man put it this way: "Plumbing fixtures are frightfully difficult to obtain; getting linoleum is sheer crucifixion!" The railroads need new freight and passenger cars, along with locomotives to replace worn out stock from the war effort. In 1946, the average freight car is twenty years old; the total number in service in 1945-6 is 50,000. No passenger cars were built in 1943 or 1944. By July 1, 596 diesel locomotives are on order for the nation's railroads, along with 94 steam locomotives for freight and 8 steamers for passenger service.

In 1946, the PRR has 10,000 fewer people on its payroll than in 1945, yet it is paying about the same amount in wages as it did a year ago. It has been taking delivery of the final locomotives in an order of fifty steam passenger T1 locomotives described in the Company's annual report as "Pennsylvania type, 4-cylinder, 4-pairs of drivers, developing sixty-five hundred horsepower." Also in the annual report, is the brief note that "one diesel electric passenger locomotive was delivered and ten more ordered." The report continued, "Those on order are the six-thousand horsepower Mountain type for through heavy passenger runs."

So, we hail 1946! And we drink to peace! We watch the great trains and wonder at the huge new locomotives. At left, prototype #6111, the only T1 with a booster, accelerates *The Admiral* out of Chicago, over the Alton Junction crossing of the Alton, C&WI, IC, and Santa Fe. The train is coming out onto the junction from the 22nd Street Bridge over the South Branch of the Chicago River, seen in the background. Other railroads have trackage rights through the junction and the operator has his hands full with his 79-lever Union Switch & Signal electro-pneumatic interlocking set up.

At upper right, the troop-laden *Liberty Limited-Second Section* rolls eastward out of Englewood. The Railroad is short of all types of equipment and several horse-express cars are in service handling storage mail. The first section of the *Liberty Limited* has the head end cars today. The K4s has received the fabricated pilot, along with the rest of the "beauty treatment." The first drop-coupler pilot was applied to K4s #5492 at Juniata in 1938, followed by the four *Jeffersonian/South Wind* streamlined K4s engines in 1940. At the lower right, an M1 rumbles eastward through Englewood, her trailing merchandise banging over the Rock Island diamonds. This is the Railroad's Chicago Terminal Division from milepost 468.4 just outside of Chicago Union Station, to Hobart, Ind., at milepost 435.1, where it becomes the Fort Wayne Division. Many of the freight trains come out of the 59th Street Yard over the 2.4 mile Englewood Connecting Line just north of Englewood to the 55th Street Freight Yard and then east on the C.T. Division. This "little" division is comprised of just under one hundred route miles through Cook County, Ill., and Lake County, Ind., but serves the important South Chicago, Gary, Mahoning, and Whiting, Ind., industrial district. There are 29 manned interlocking and/or block stations on its trackage. (Harley)

All gentlemen's agreements and tacit understandings between the Pennsylvania and New York Central come to an end when two of their trains arrive at, or around, the same time in Englewood, headed east. Much more than the reputation of man and machine is at stake in each race. On occasions, the Nickel Plate gets into the act with Pennsy, as its trains use the Central's tracks through Englewood east to Grand Crossing and their access to the IC. Below is No. 8 leaving town behind L-1a class Hudson #173, without a PRR train in sight. At right, Central's magnificent diesel-fighting Niagara shows us what 6600 horses can do with the *20th Century Limited* out of Englewood. Almost out of sight is the through West Coast sleeper off the *California Zephyr*. At lower right, Rock Island's westbound *Golden State Limited* is about to bang across the diamonds at Englewood. Both the 4000 horsepower E7s on Rock Island and the New

York Central S-1 Niagara were built in 1945, representing the pinnacle of the builder's art. All four railroads share one station, while the interlocking plant is Rock Island's, with the PRR sharing the expenses. The electro-mechanical interlocking plant features a 100-lever S & F machine with an 80-bar locking bed. (Tatnall; Lloyd; Ball Collection; Ball)

We are just about a minute out of Chicago Union Station, standing on Roosevelt Road looking south over the numerous tracks in and out of Union. The Pennsylvania's vast 12th Street coach yard is seen in the background. Far off in the distance are the bascule bridges of the IC's St. Charles Air Line and the B&O Chicago Terminal leads to Grand Central Station, over the South Branch of the Chicago River.

A fitting close to our journey is the 3:00 departure and beginning of another journey, of the elegant *California Zephyr* bound for the great American west and a 2,532-mile crossing to the Pacific. Western Pacific's vista-dome sleeper-buffet lounge-observation car, "Silver Crescent," brings up the rear. At lower left, and ten minutes later, PRR's train No. 71 heads into Union with head end cars, a P-70, and a P-82 from Richmond, Ind., and the connection off *The Spirit of St. Louis*. Above, and a few minutes past 5:00 PM, a vision of tuscan and delux yellow glides past in the personage of the all-Pullman room *Broadway Limited* to New York. Observation car "Mountain View" brings up the rear with its two master rooms, double bedroom, and buffet lounge. Ahead, are cars with every configuration of double bedrooms, roomettes, and duplex single rooms. The lounge car, "Harbor Rest," with its five double-bed-rooms and trainphone is toward the center, next to twin-unit dining car 4622-4623.

One half hour earlier, the throaty voice of over 6000 horsepower worth of V-12 diesels could clearly be heard roaring out of LaSalle Street Station on the *20th Century*. Both trains will arrive in New York at 9:30 AM, however, as the *Broadway* will make the run in 15½ hours, cutting a half hour off the *Century's* 16-hour schedule. (Tatnall)

203

According to PRR promotional brochures, "Here, The West Begins!" For us, here in Chicago is where we take leave of the Pennsy, at bumper post's end at Chicago Union Station, 907.7 miles from Pennsylvania Station in New York. EMD is now firmly in command. The Burlington units have come in from Denver, 1,034 miles away; the GM&O is up from St. Louis, 283.9 miles to the south; and, of course, our EP-22s are in from Harrisburg, 713.1 miles to the east.

The station, the largest in Chicago, was opened on July 23, 1925, and is half owned by the Pennsylvania, with the Milwaukee and Burlington each owning 25 percent. The Gulf, Mobile & Ohio is just a tenant. There are fourteen tracks on the south side of the station for the Pennsy, GM&O, and Burlington. The Milwaukee uses ten on the north side of the concourse. Three tracks run through on the east side to connect with the north.

I cannot hide the fact that visions of more adventurous times come to me—times when the chisel-flanked T1s and the burly K4s frequented Union. So, too, the "big engine" and the steam turbine that came in occasionally, heading up their seemingly endless trains of tuscan red cars. Union Station brings back memories of S-1 and S-2 Pacifics on Q's commuter trains, too, along with the great 3000 class Hudsons and silver diesels that headed up the long distance trains. To many, Union rekindles days when the Alton came in with maroon and red Pacifics and, yes, the newer B&O diesels. On the north end of Union, of course, is the Milwaukee Road with its reminder to many of the great orange and maroon loco- motives and trains that came in and out.

Looking at the diesels, I have to ask, wasn't it just *yesterday* that dirty, friendly overall-covered men got down off their great, black engines to look 'em over, hot off the run? And was it not just yesterday that smoke filled the ceiling area down at the southerly side of the platforms under the Post Office? The incessant ringing of bells, the clank and rumble of hissing loco- motives coming in and backing out. *Wasn't it just yesterday!* (Tatnall)